A WORLD OF COLOR AND DEPTH

The Photographic Artwork of Northridge Photography

Northridge Photography thanks you for your support.

If you enjoy our work, please feel free to contact us at NorthridgePhotography@yahoo.com and be sure to check out our nature-themed, educational series: *Northridge Photography Presents*.

All images are property of Northridge Photography, and may not be used in any way without the consent of Northridge Photography.

©2018

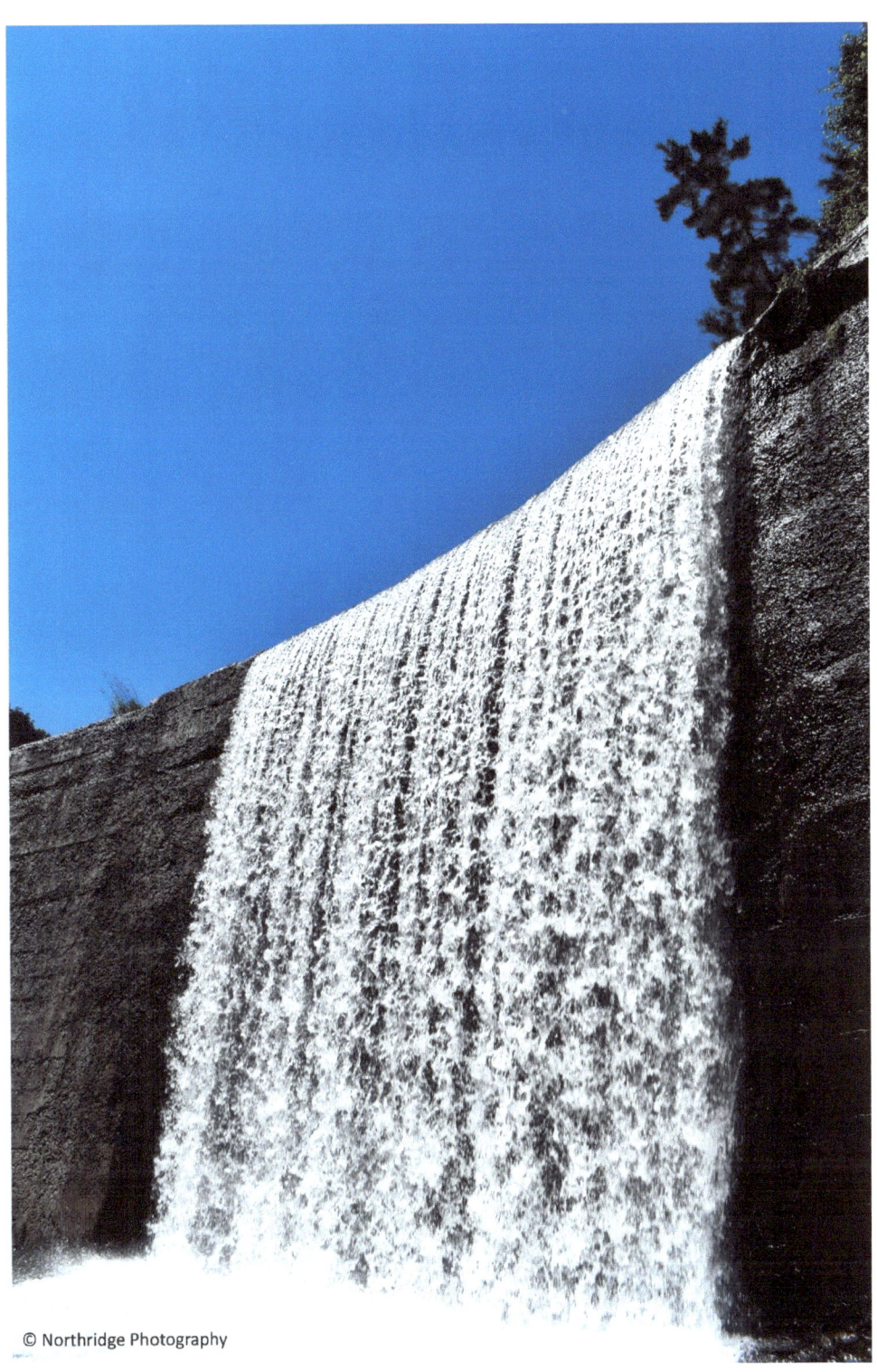

Dam at Wiscoy Falls

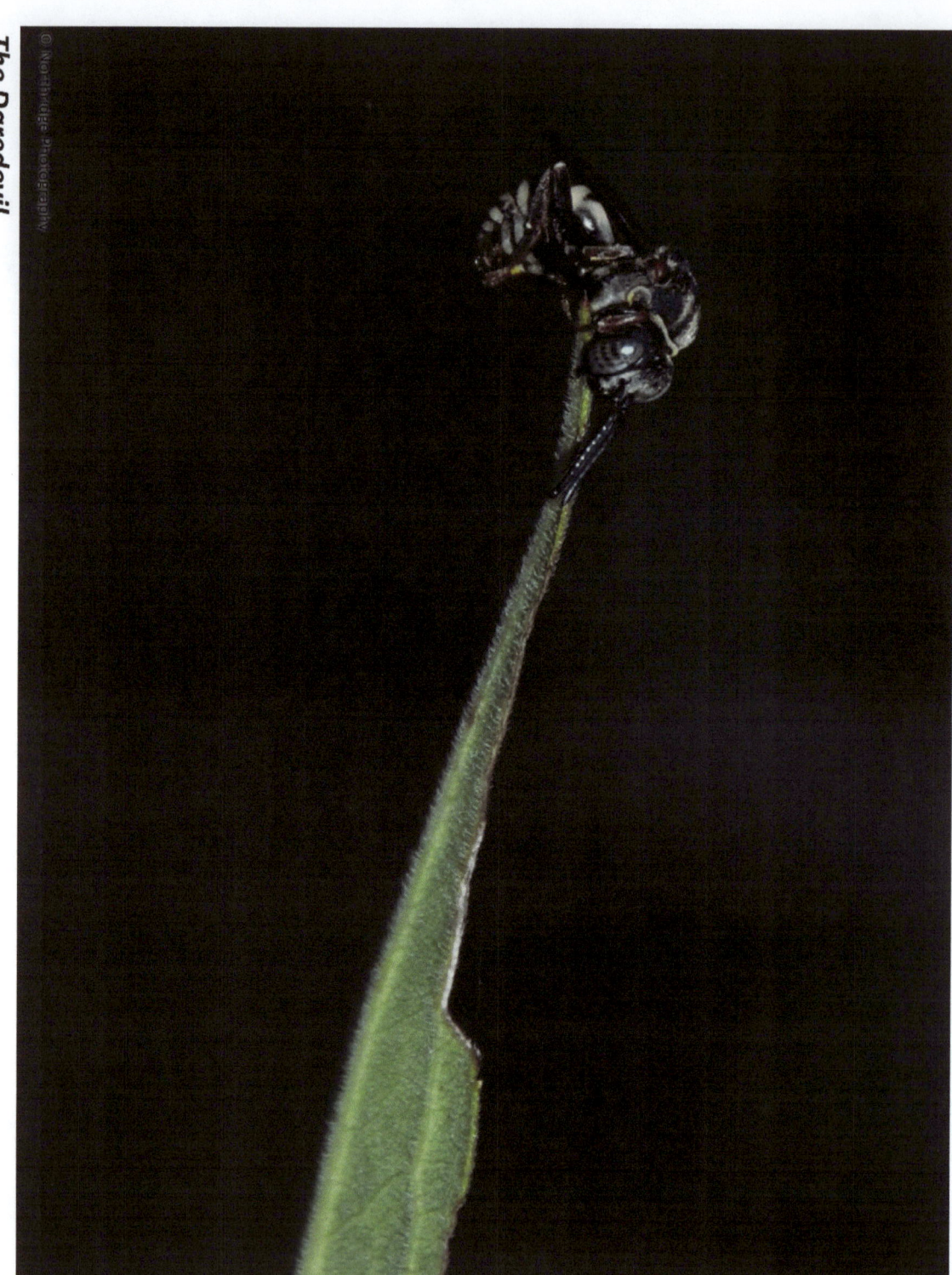

The Daredevil

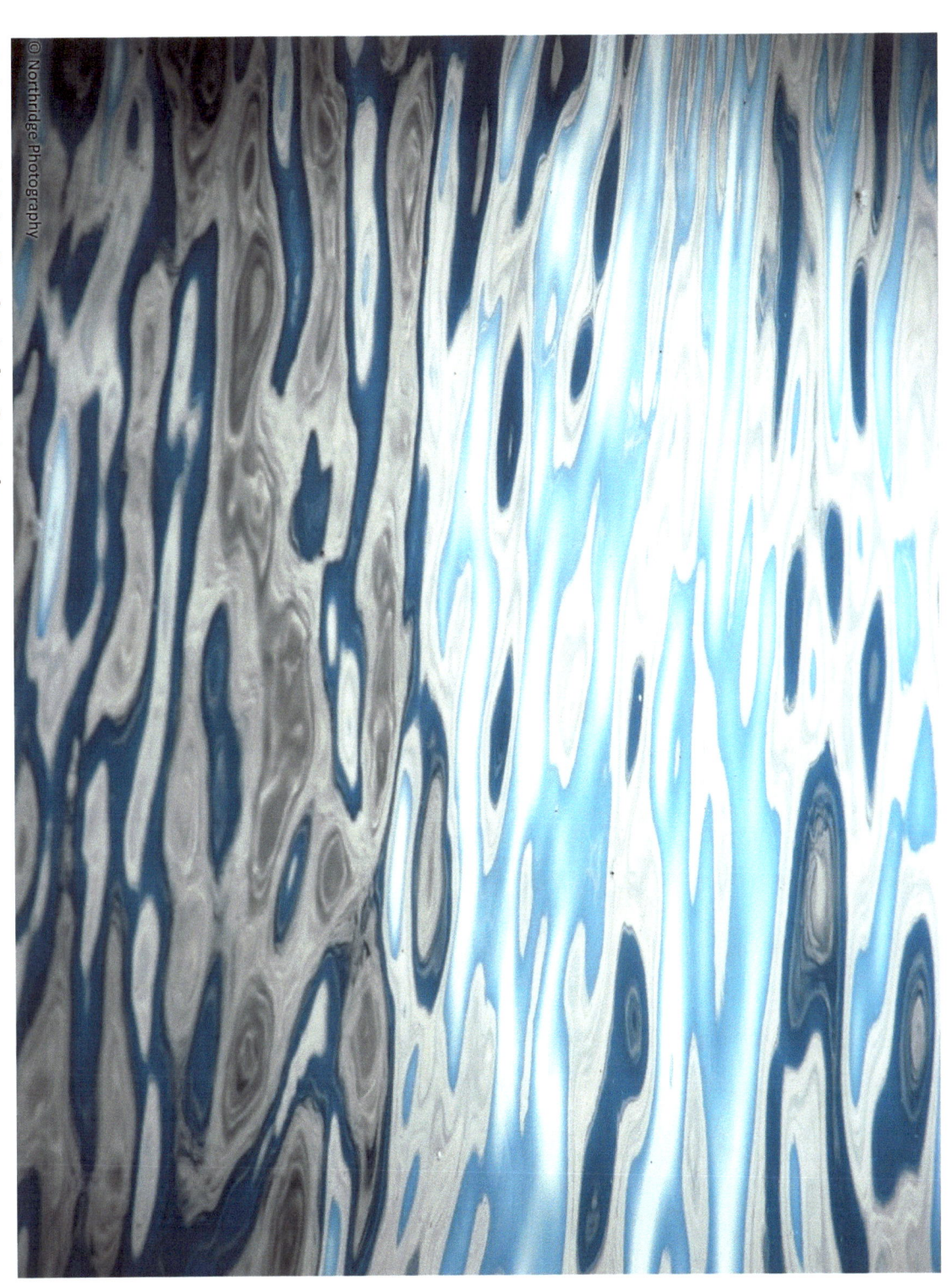

Color and Light-Study; Lake Ontario © Northbridge Photography

Spectrum

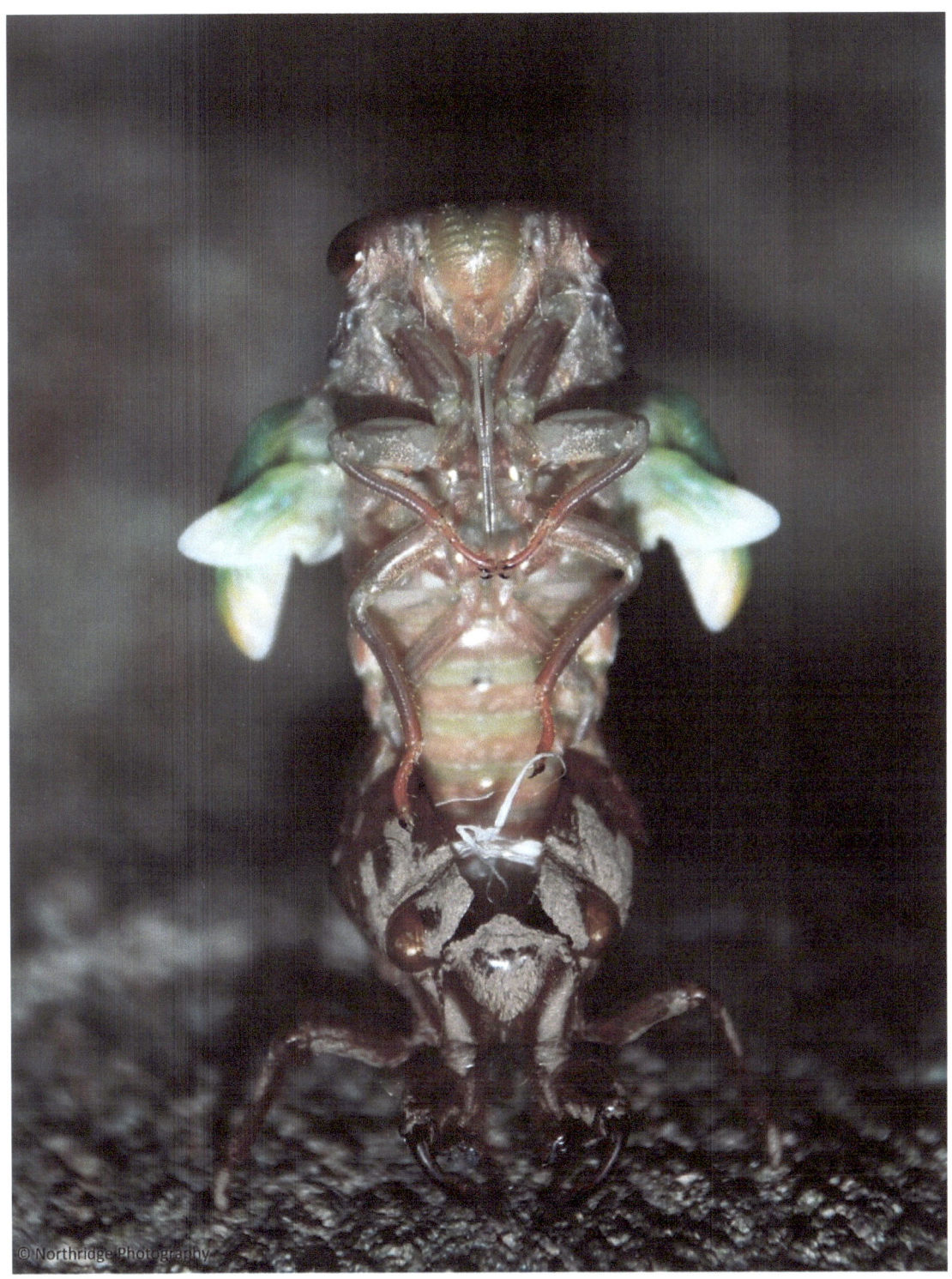

Emergence

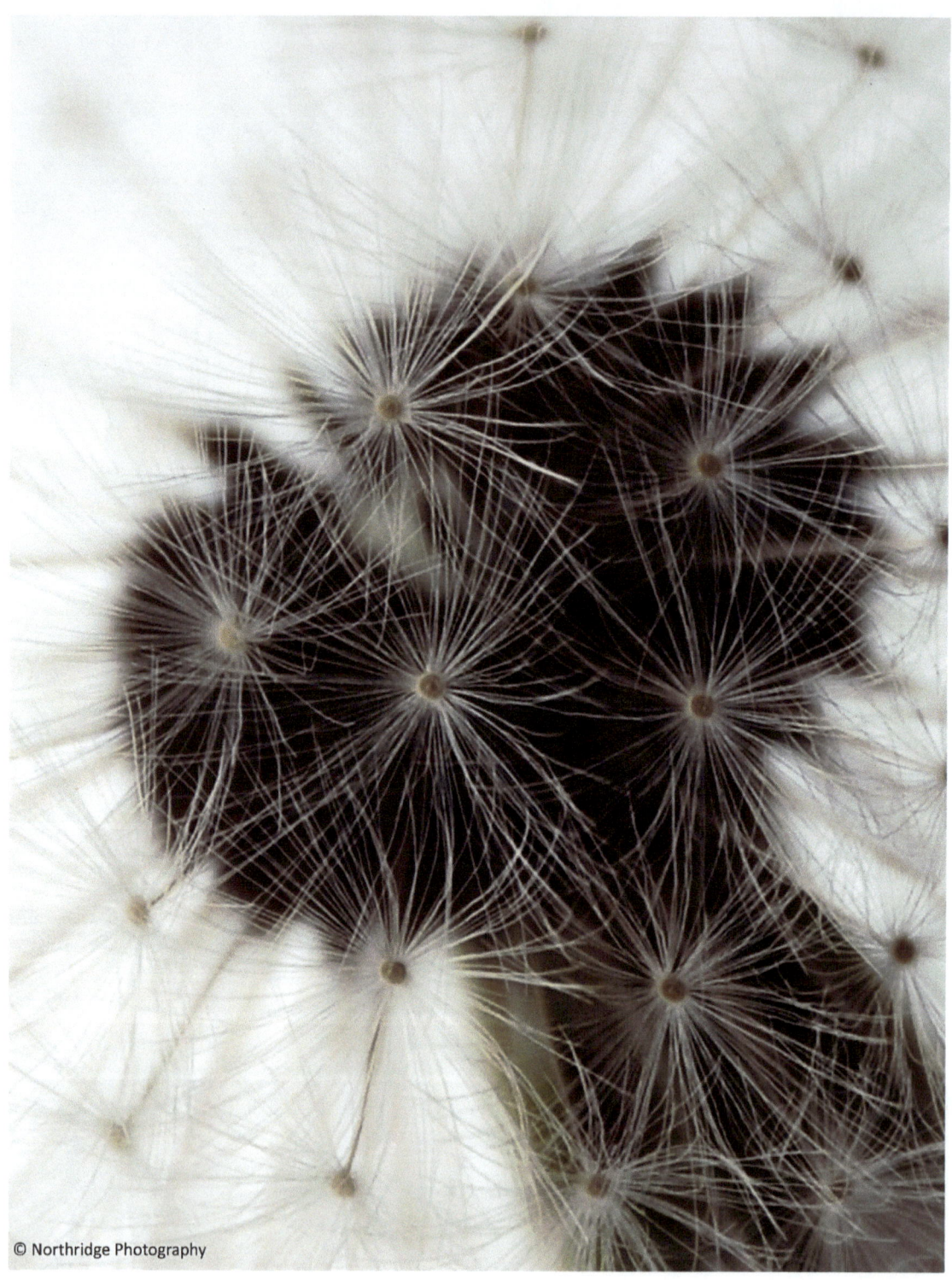

Gone to Seed

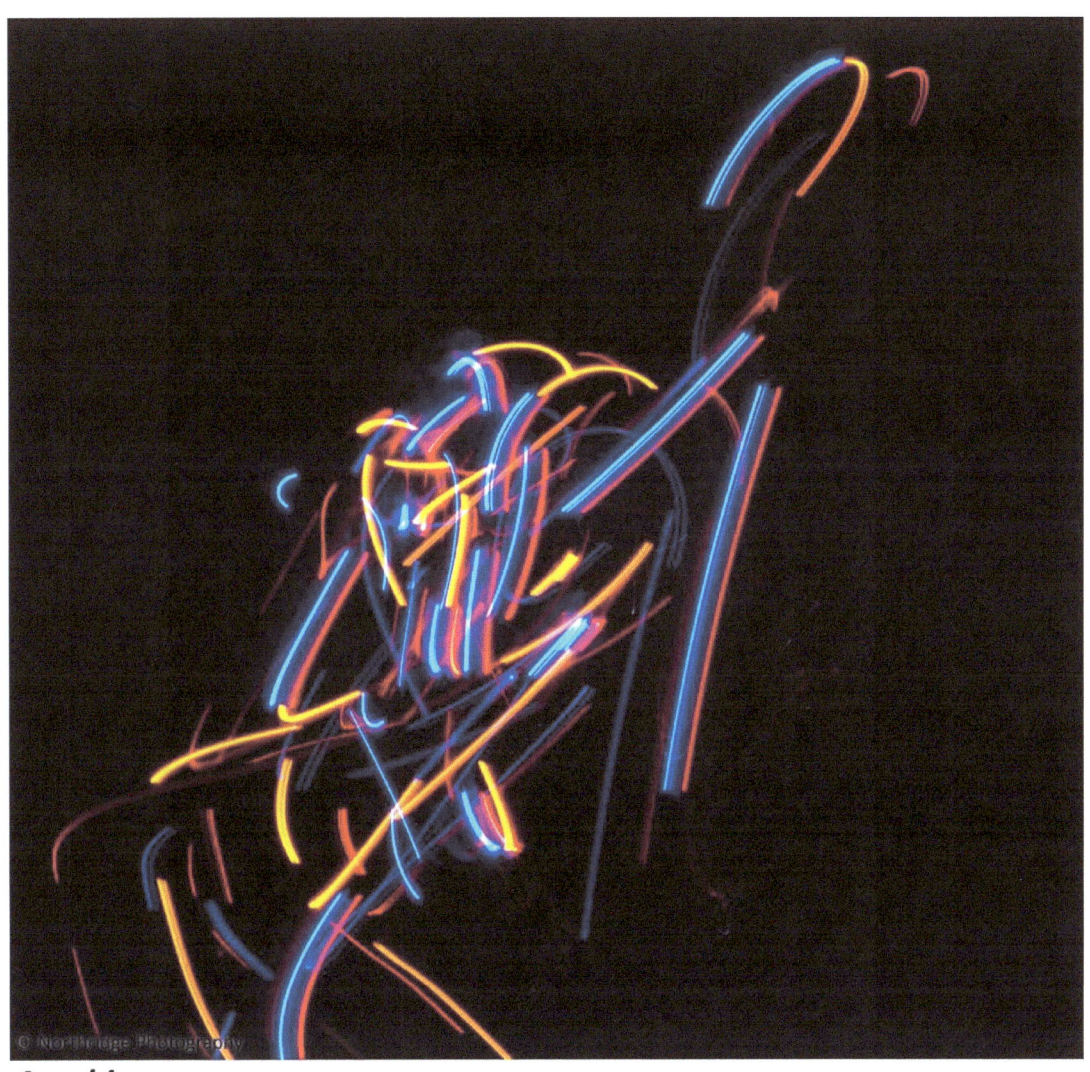

Aerobics

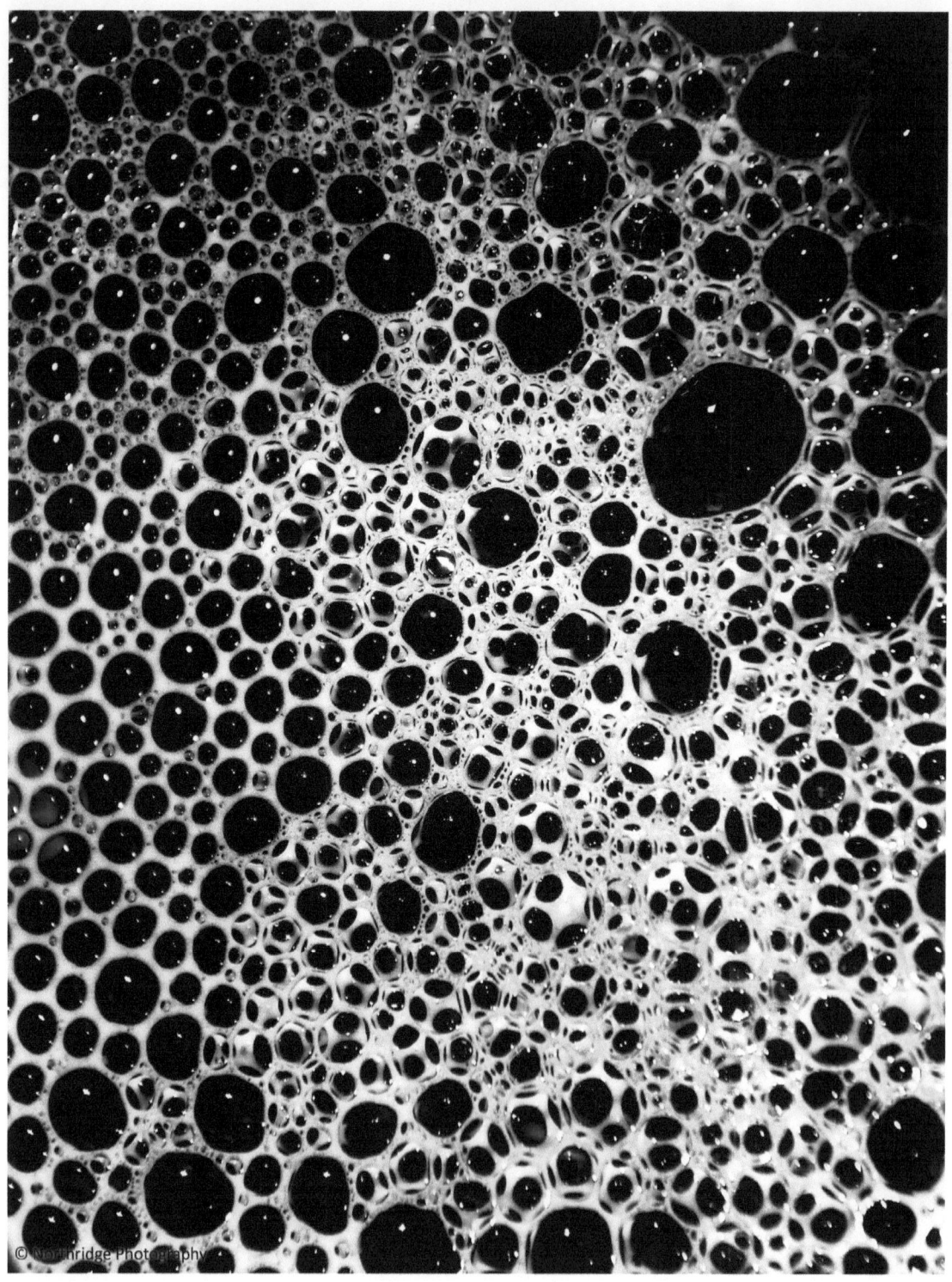

Dishsoap

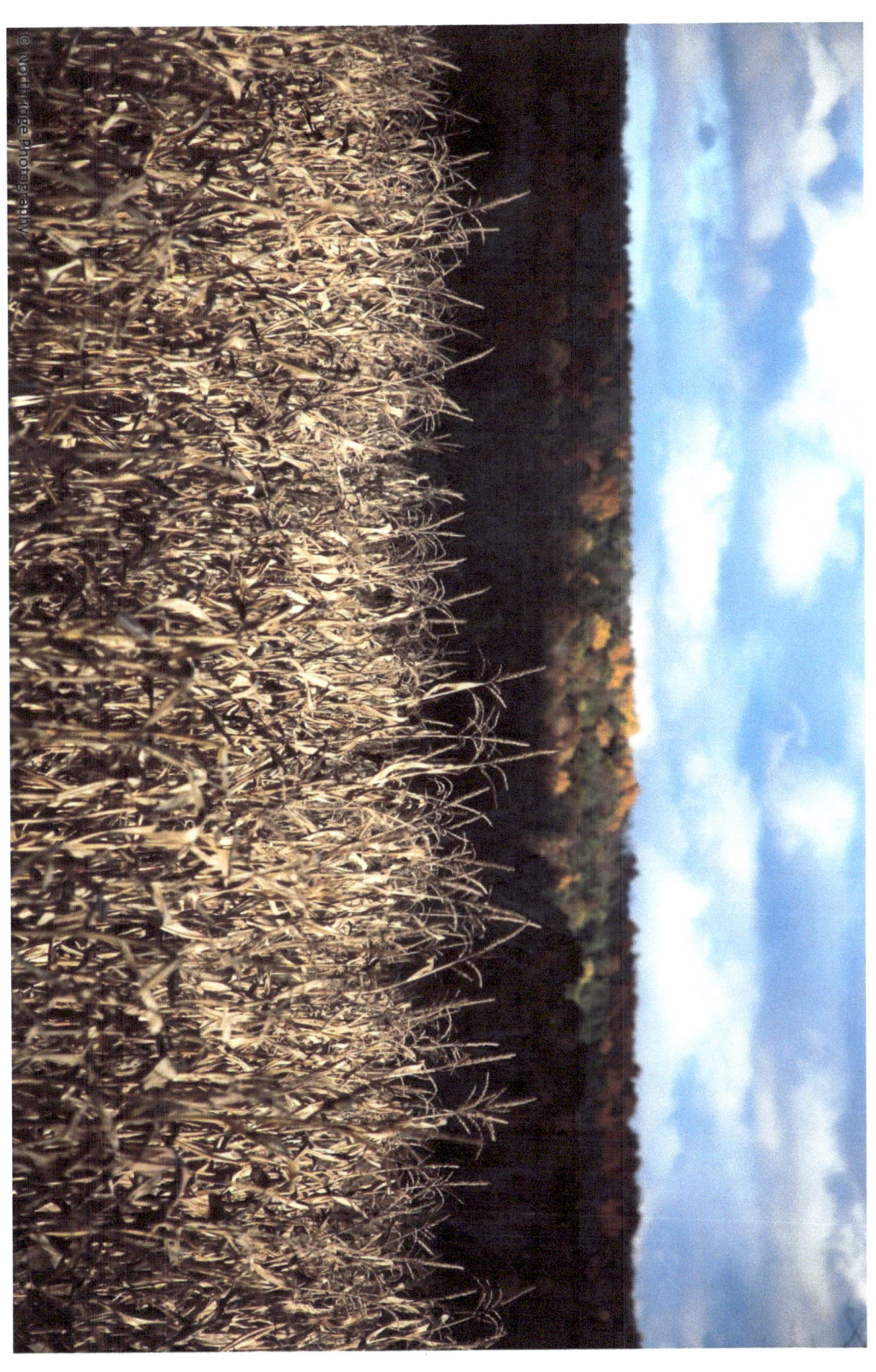

Autumn Scene

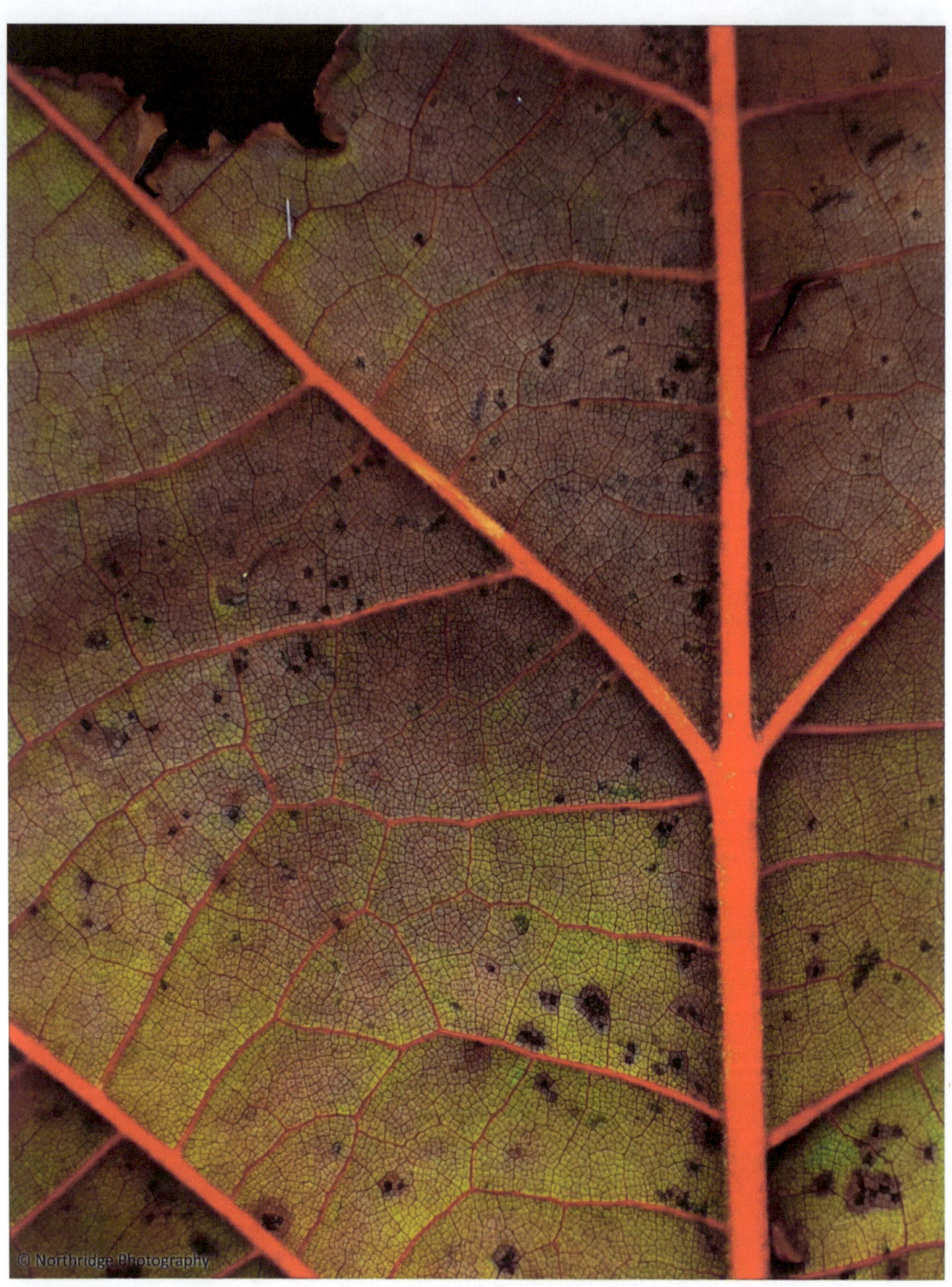

Constructal Law

Here I Stand

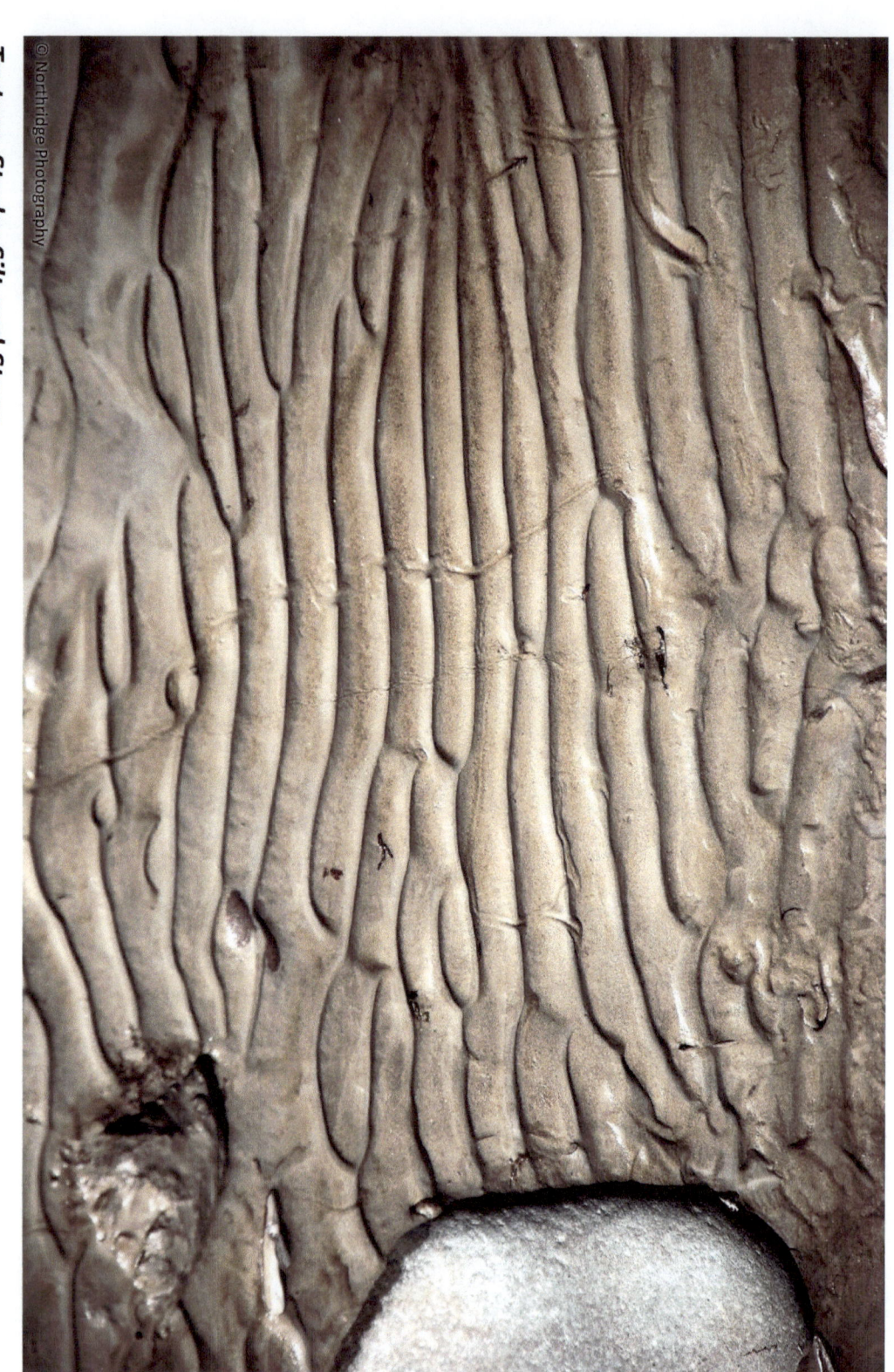

Texture-Study: Silt and Stone
© Northridge Photography

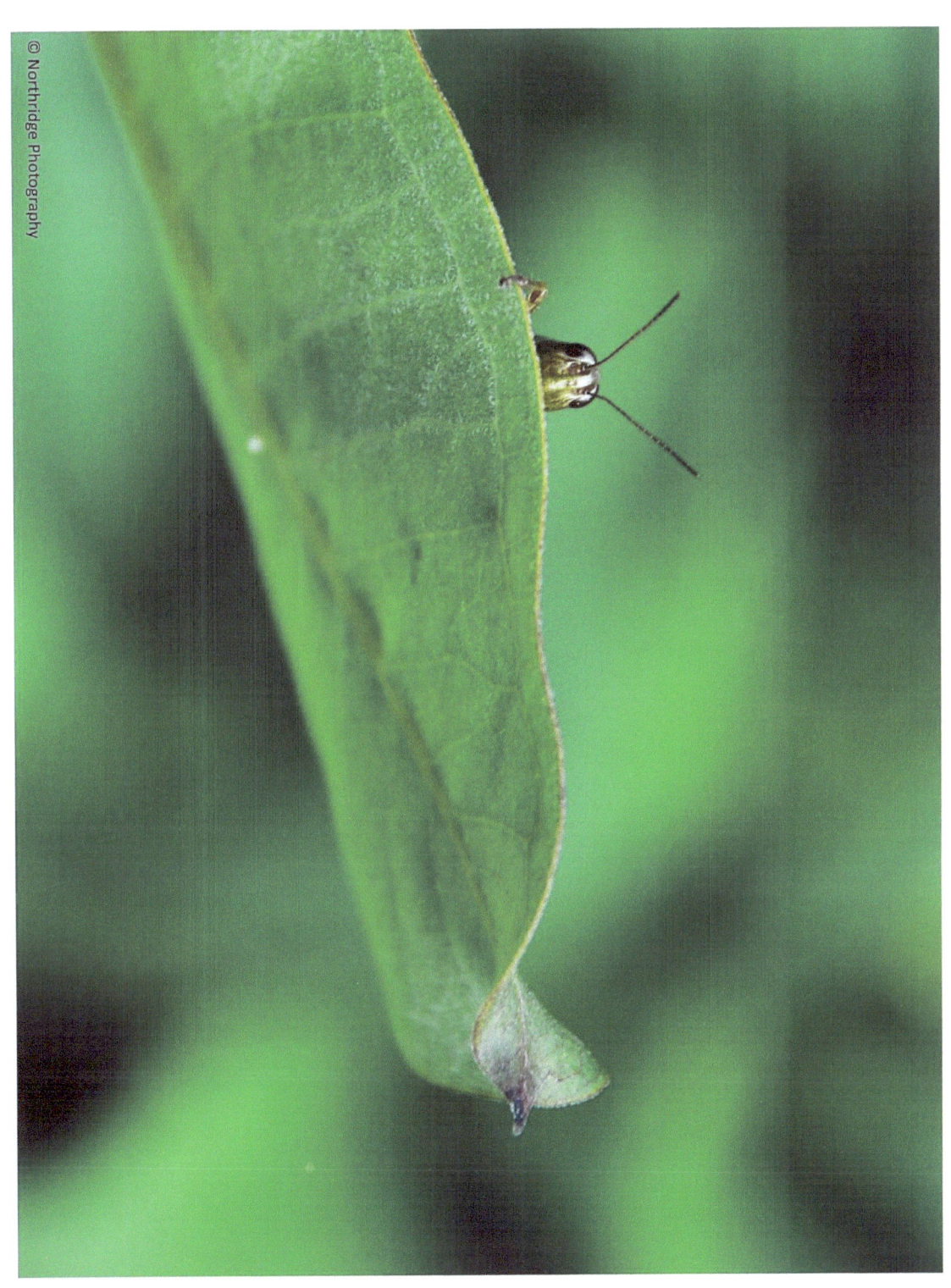

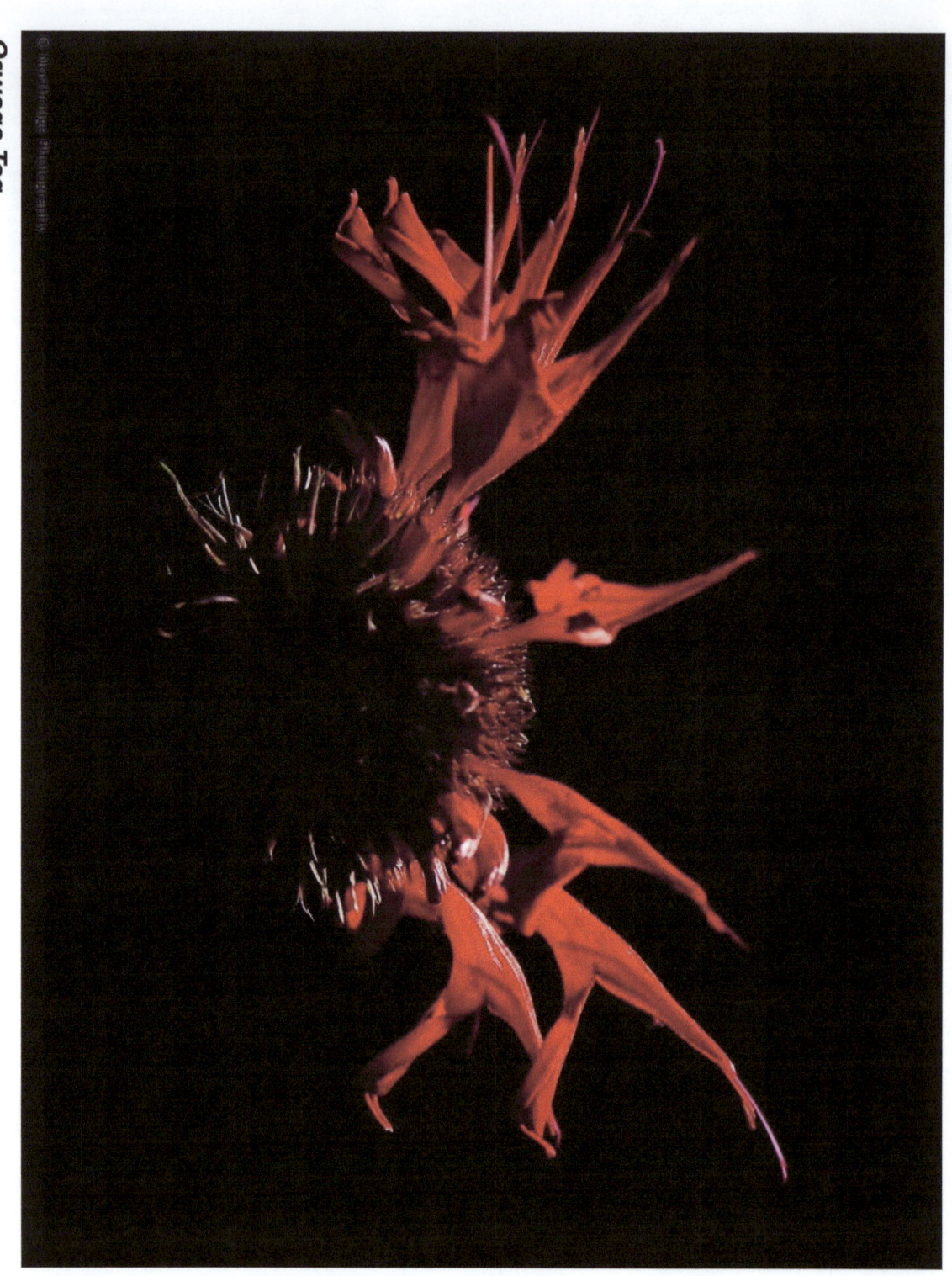
Oswego Tea

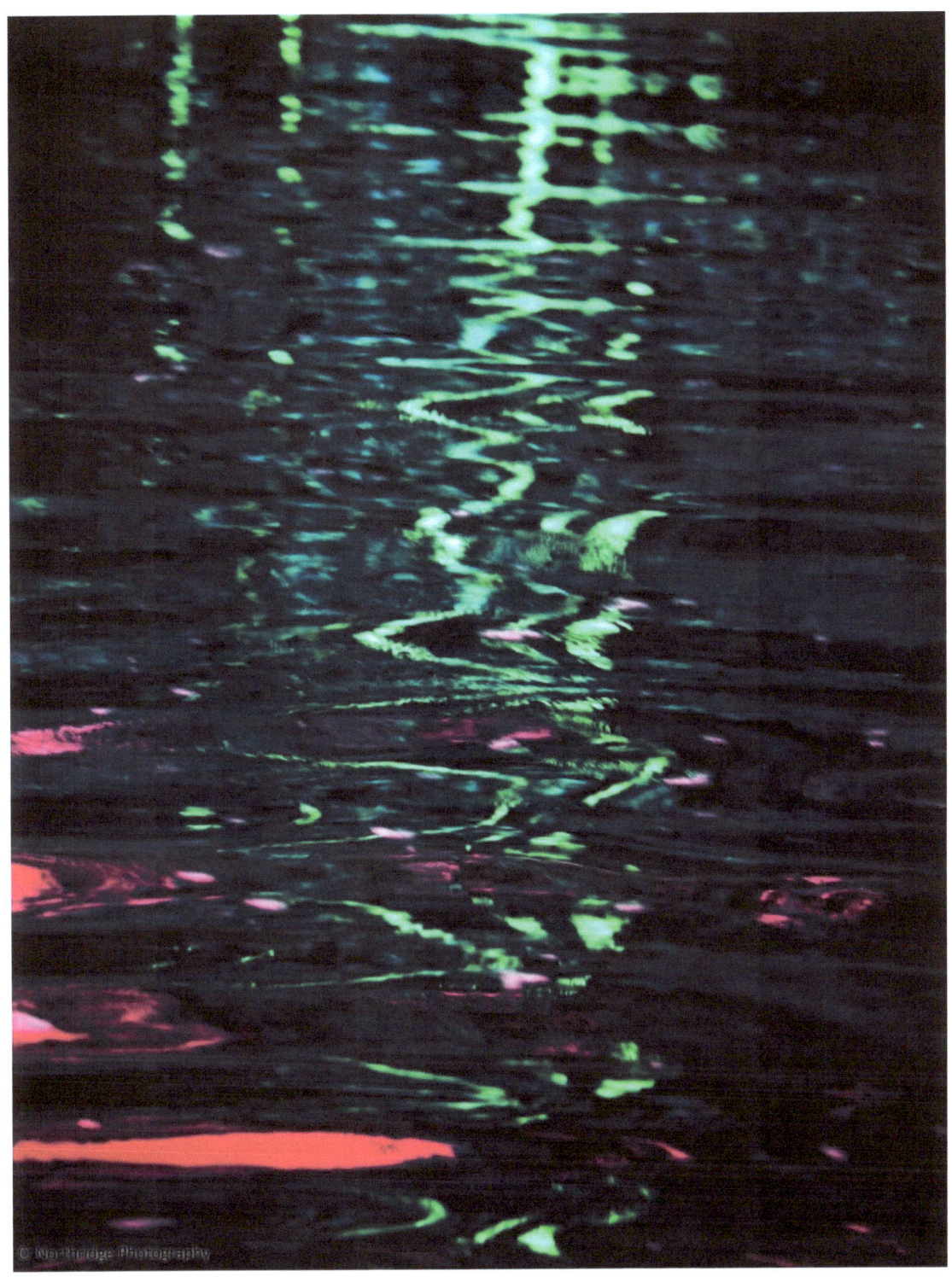

City Lights

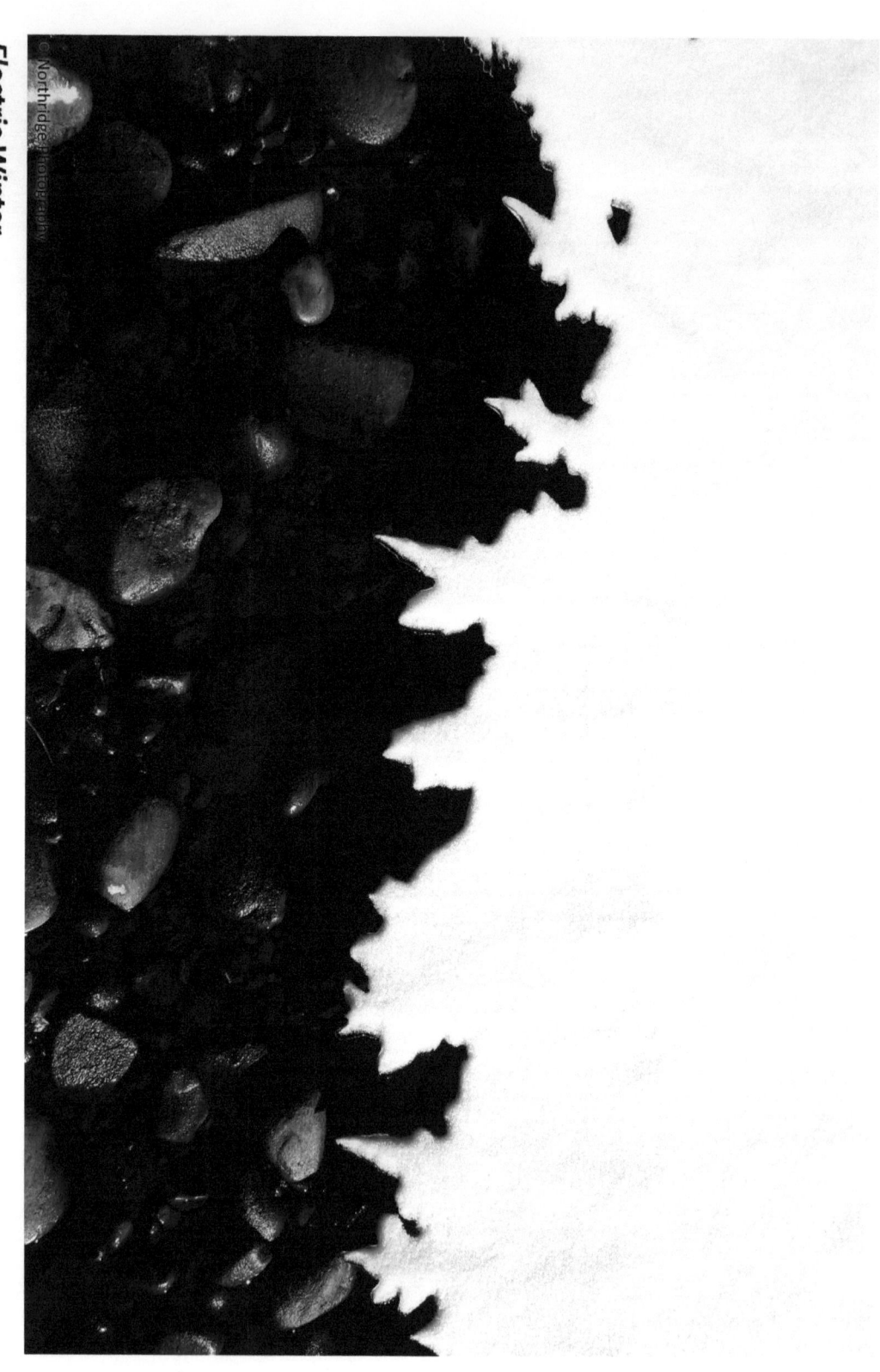
Electric Winter

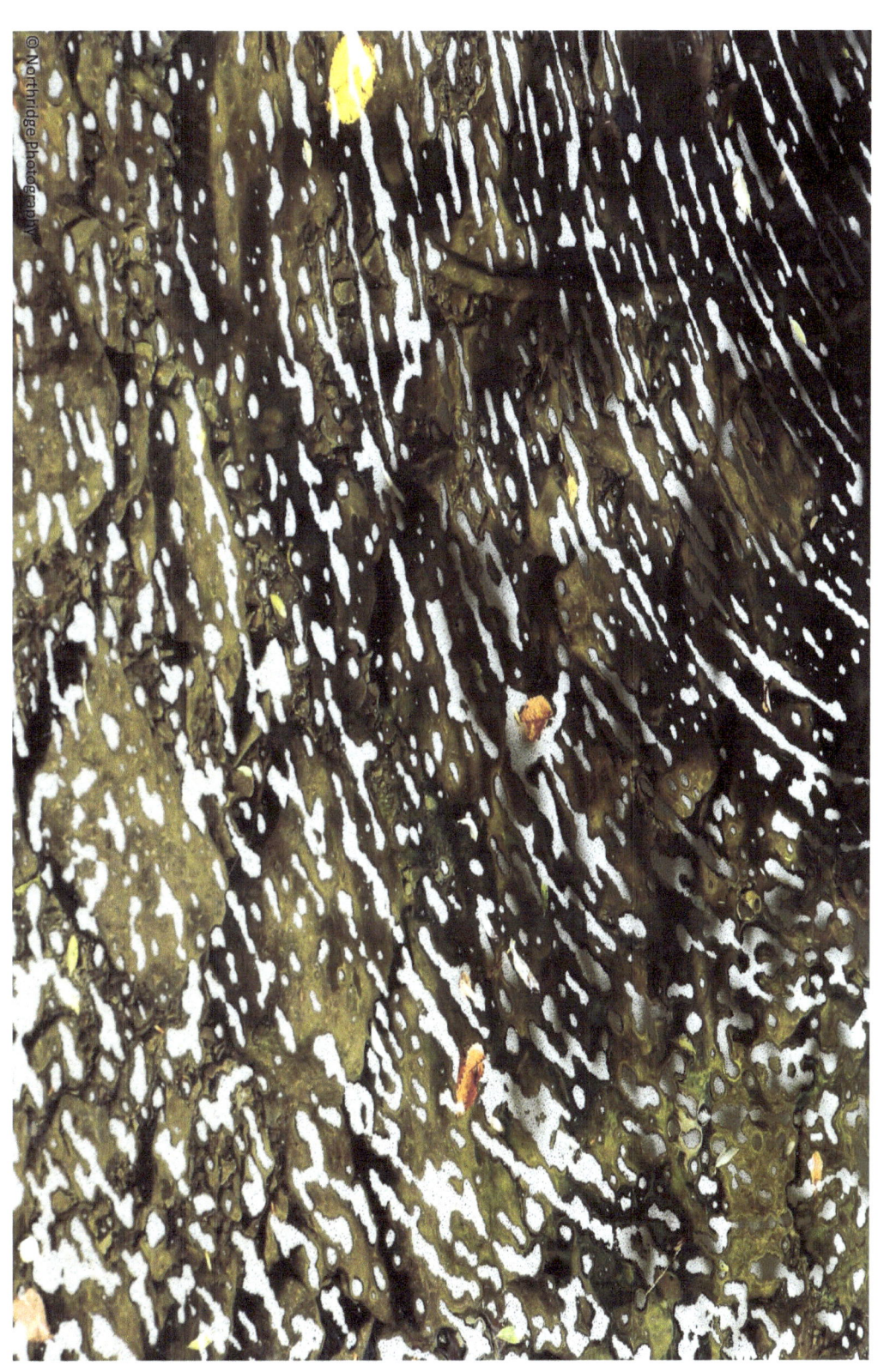

Pattern-Study; Foam and Leaves on Water

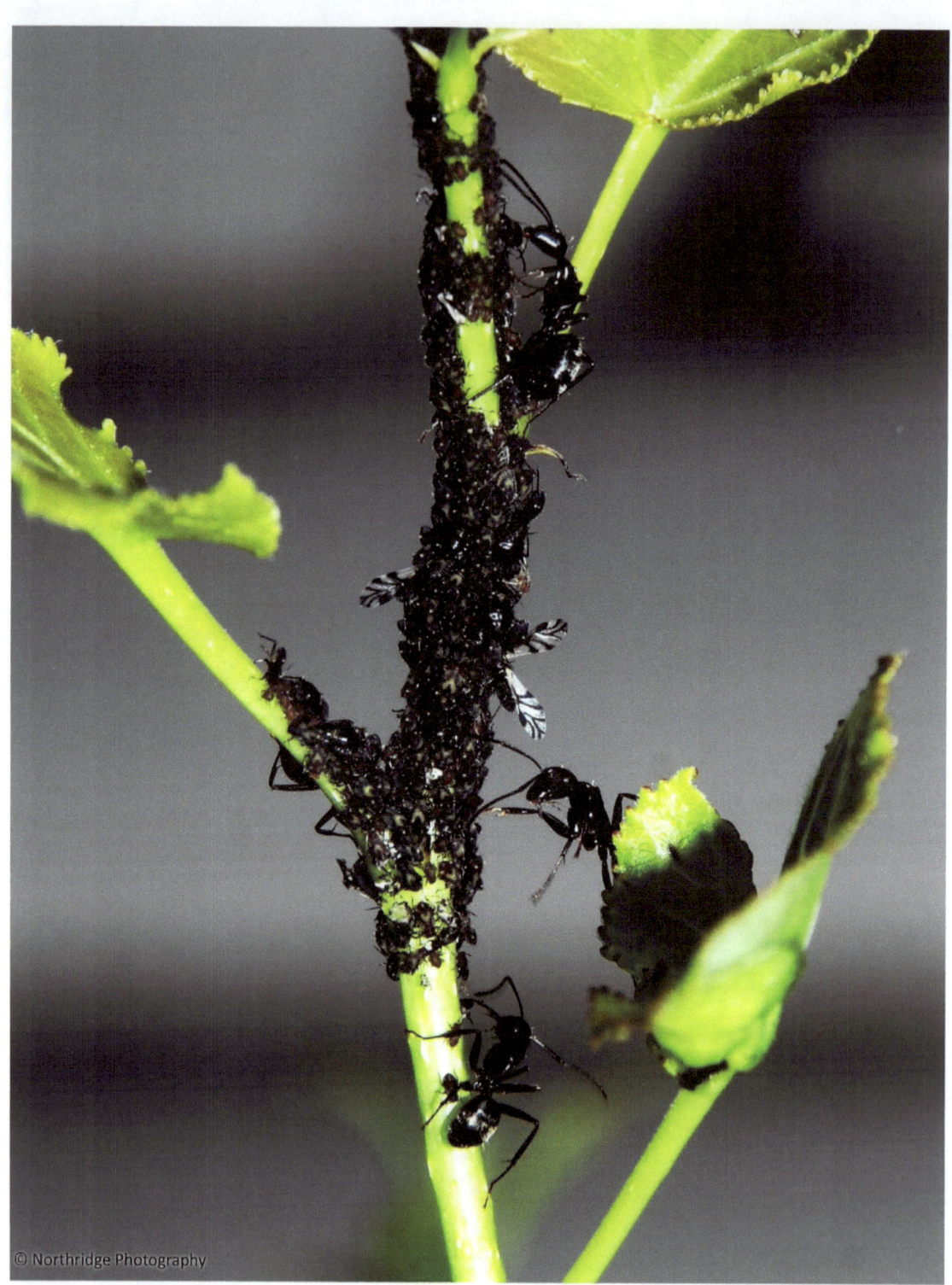

Ants and Aphids

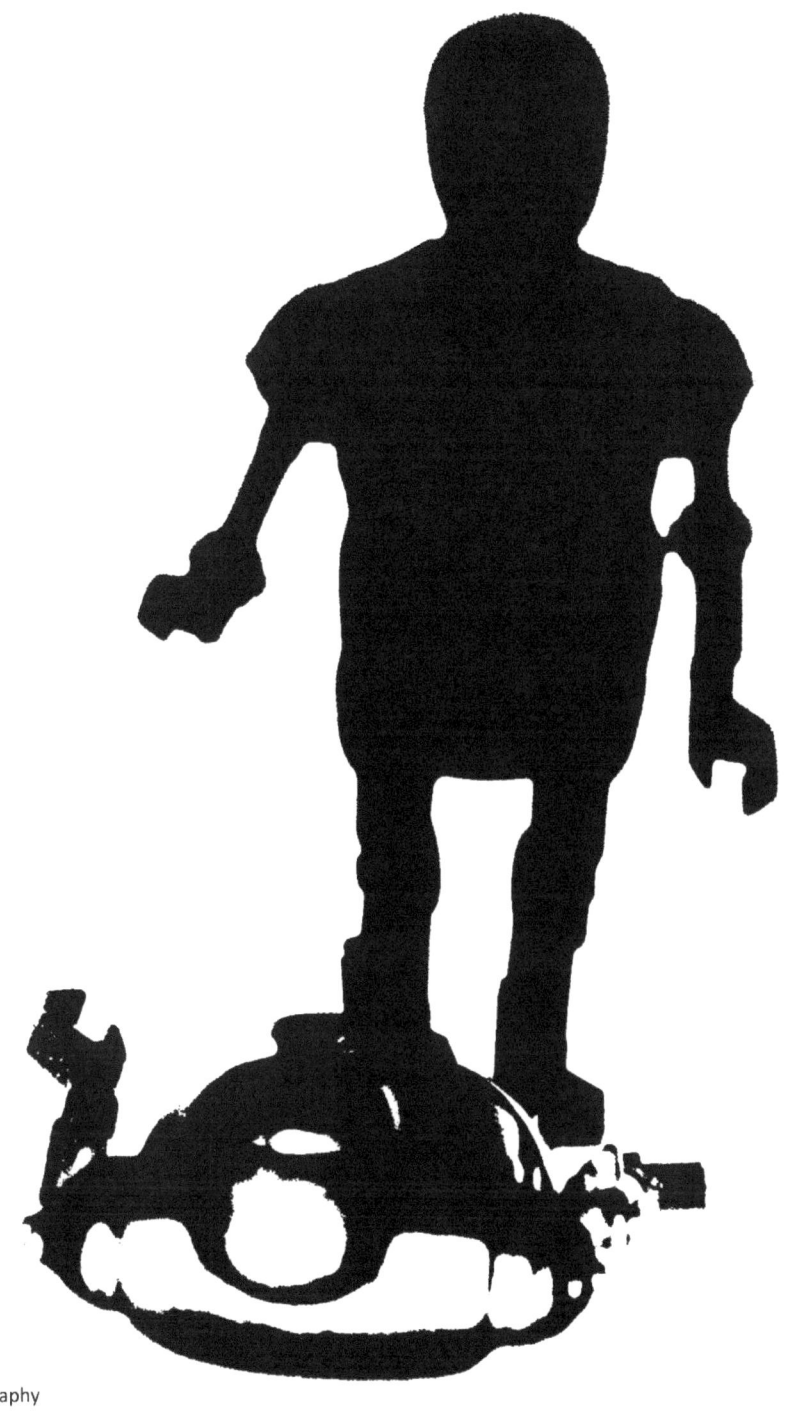

© Northridge Photography

Robot

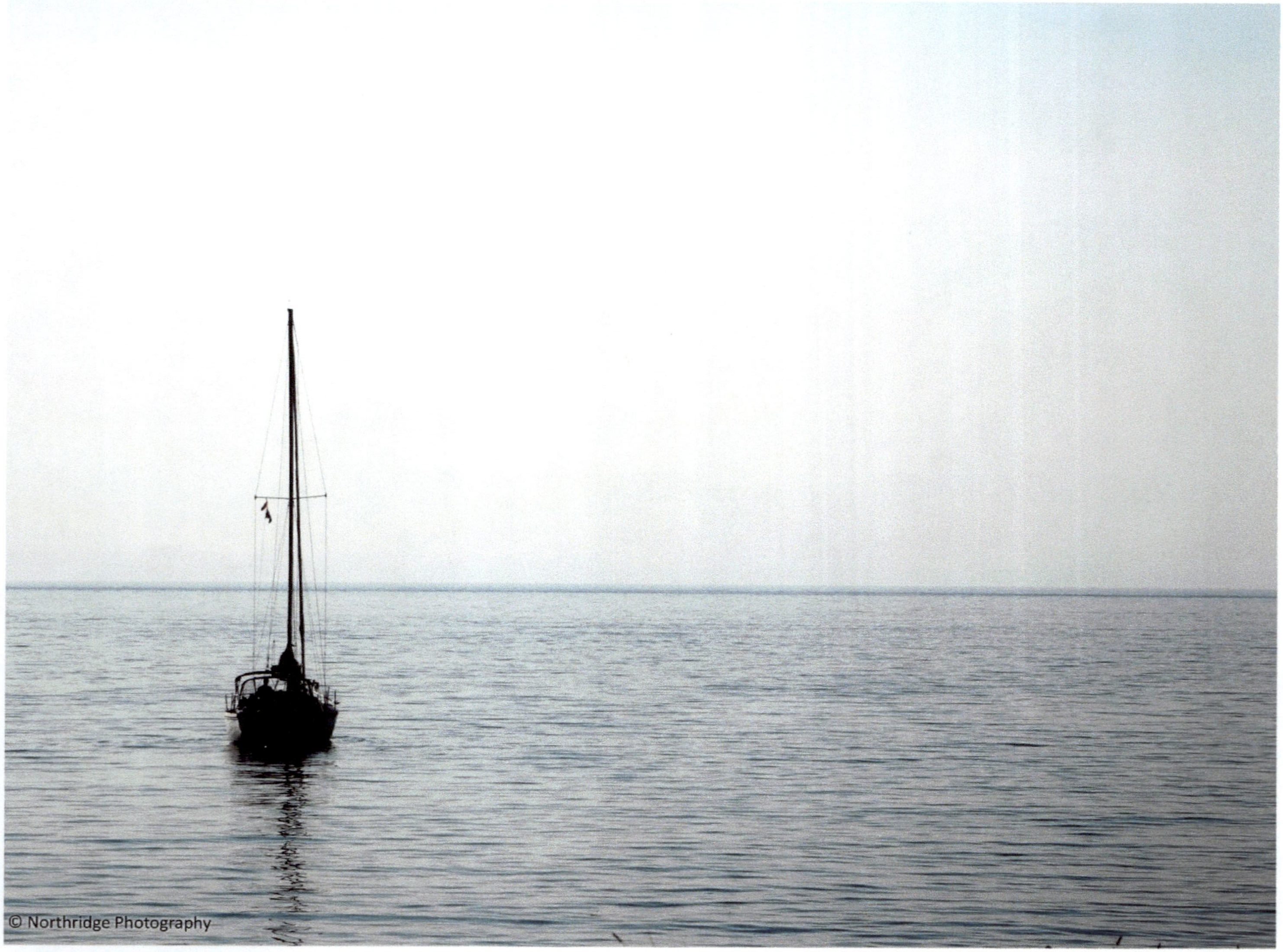

Out on the Weekend

© Northridge Photography

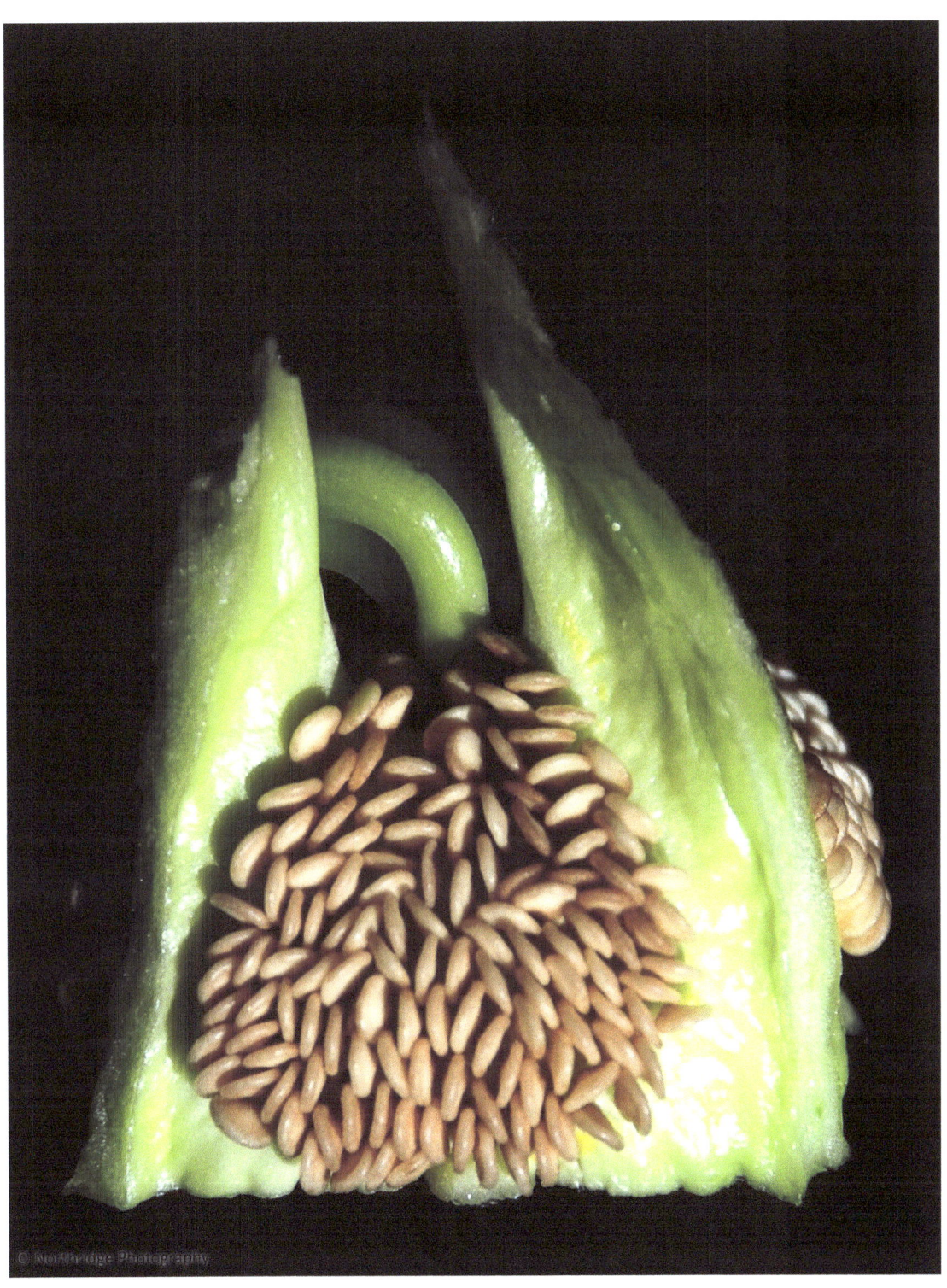

Greenbell Deconstructed

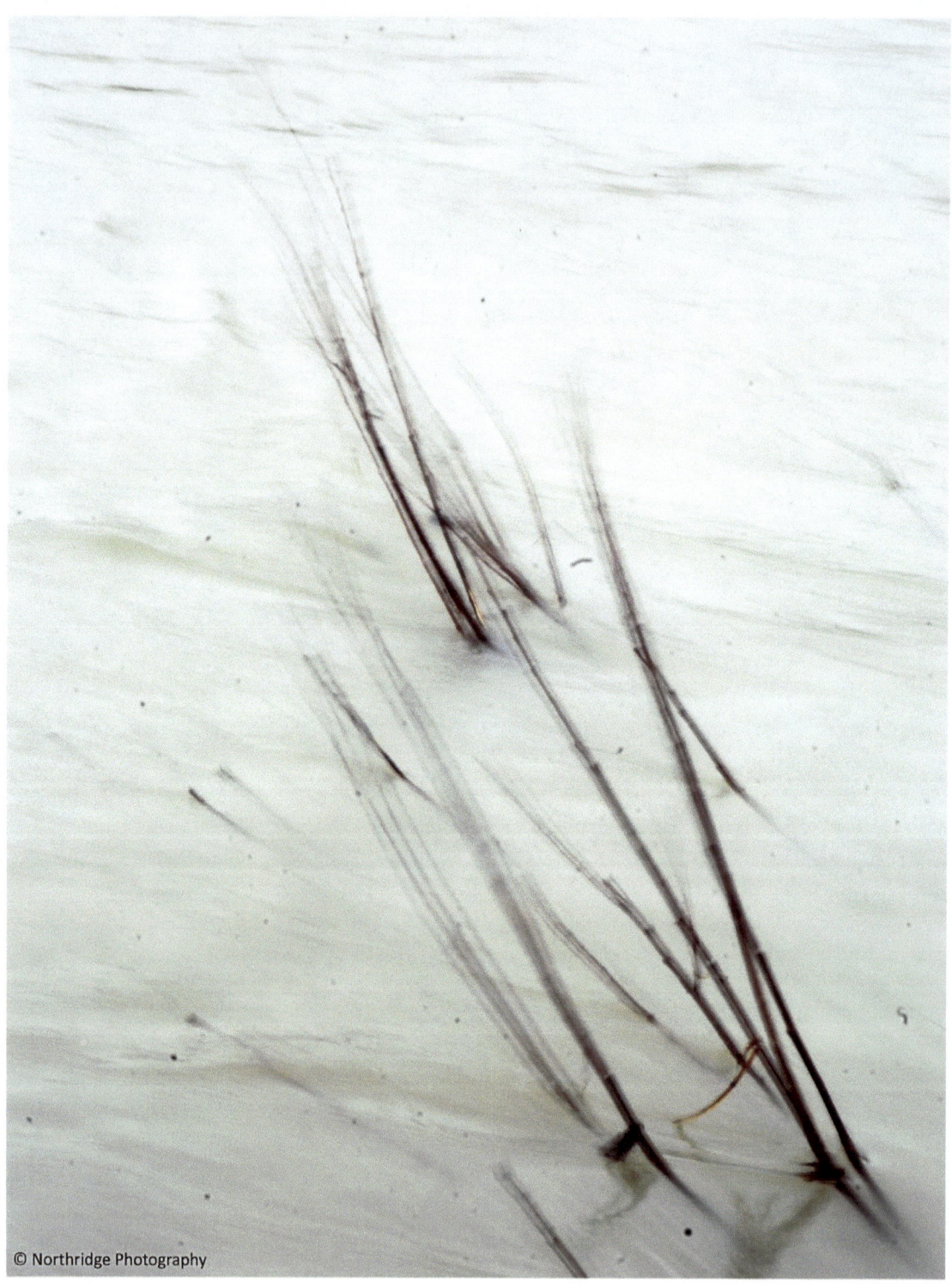

Brushstrokes

Colony © Northridge Photography

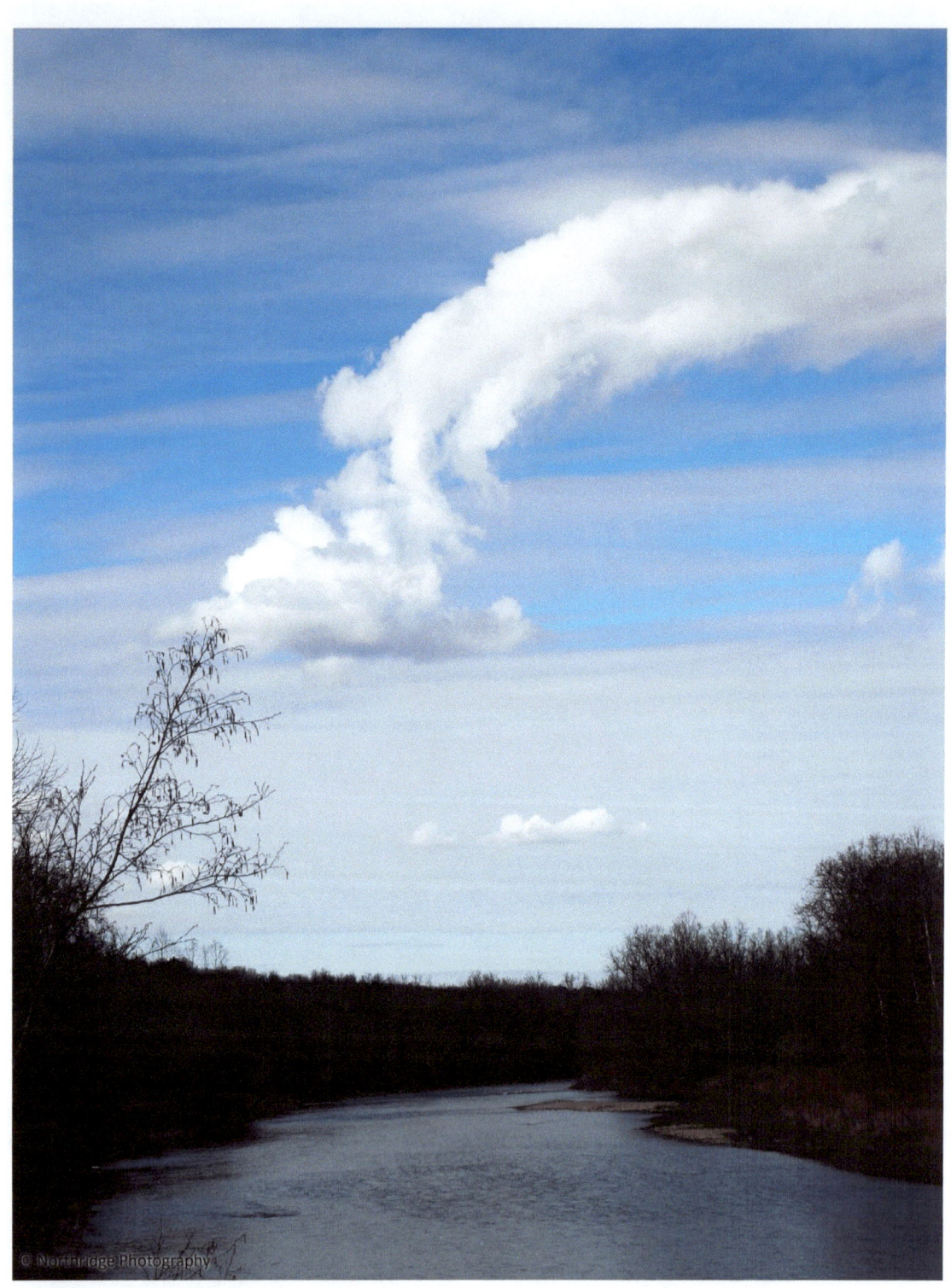

Smoke Signal Over the Genesee

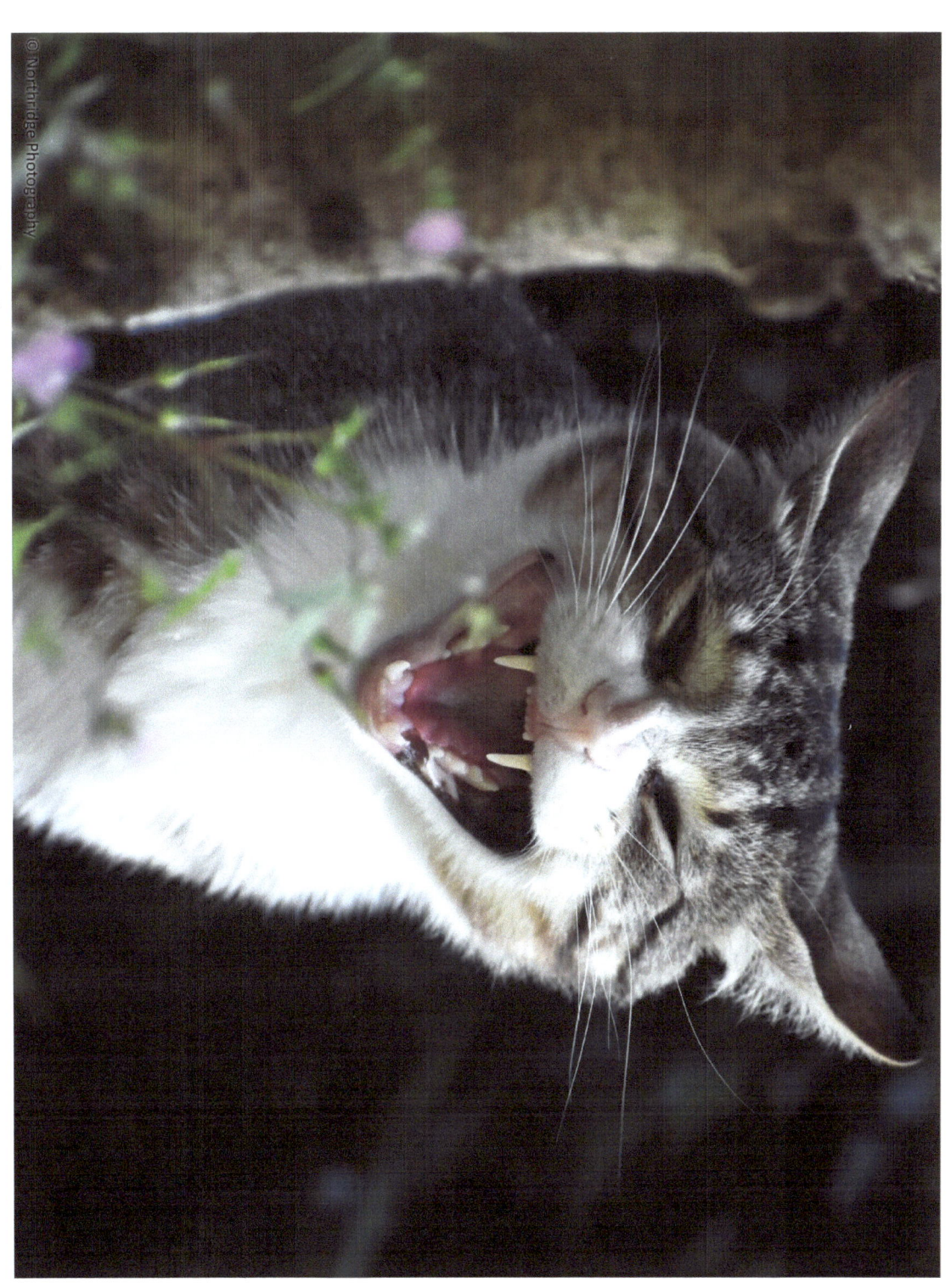

We Call Him 'Smiley' © Northridge Photography

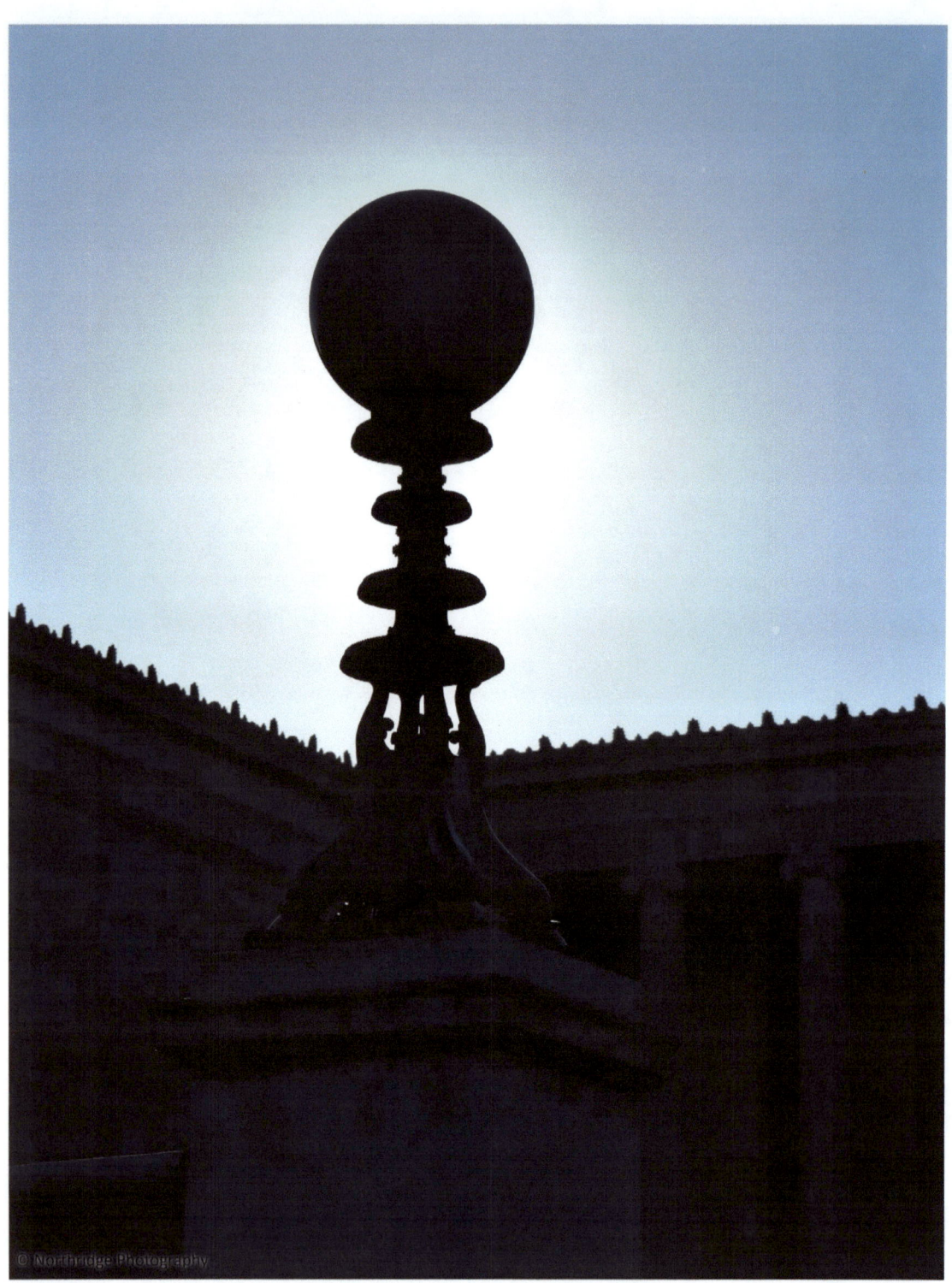

Eclipse

Enchanted © Northridge Photography

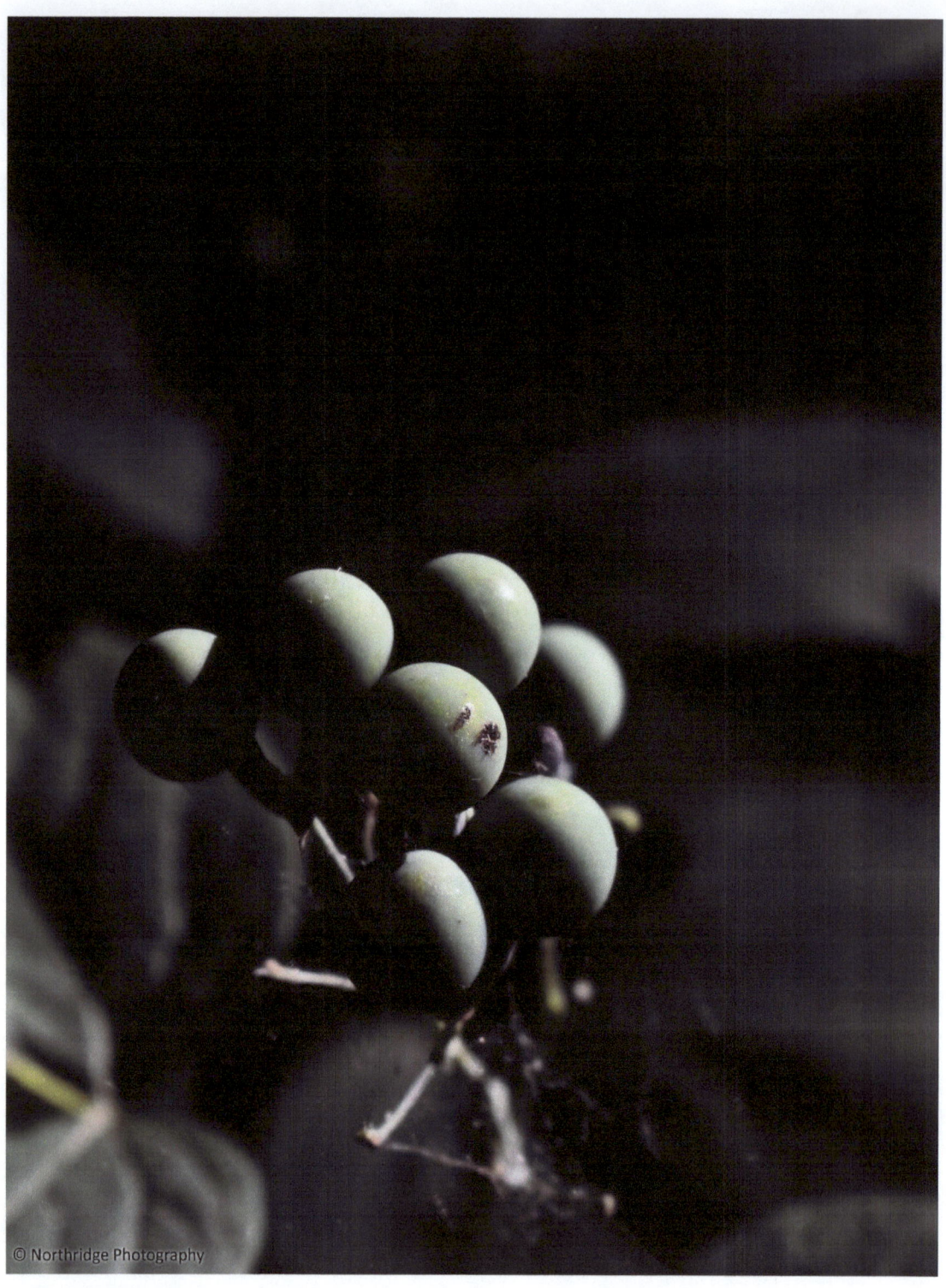

Planetary

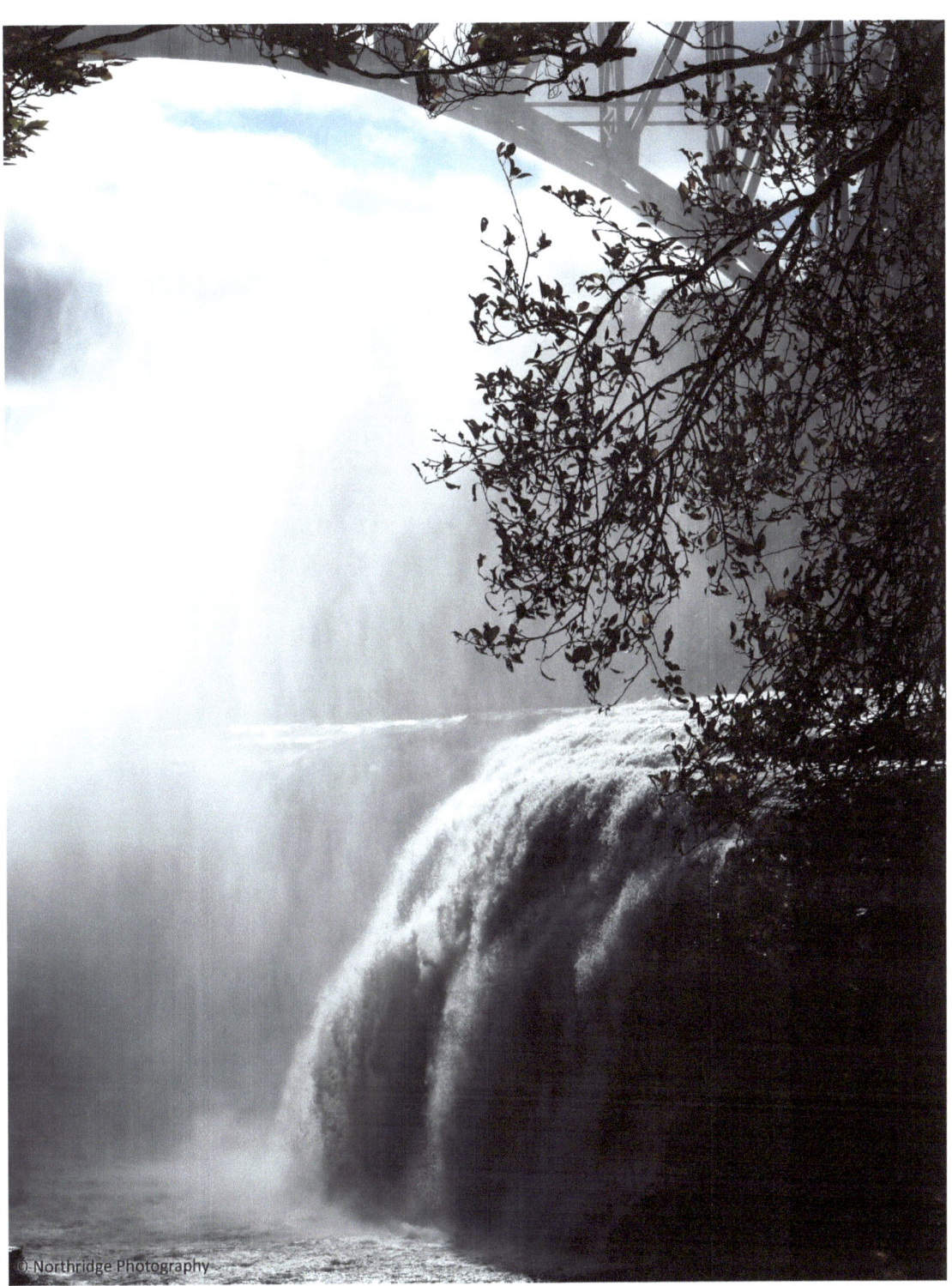

The Falls at Letchworth

Strangers

© Northridge Photography

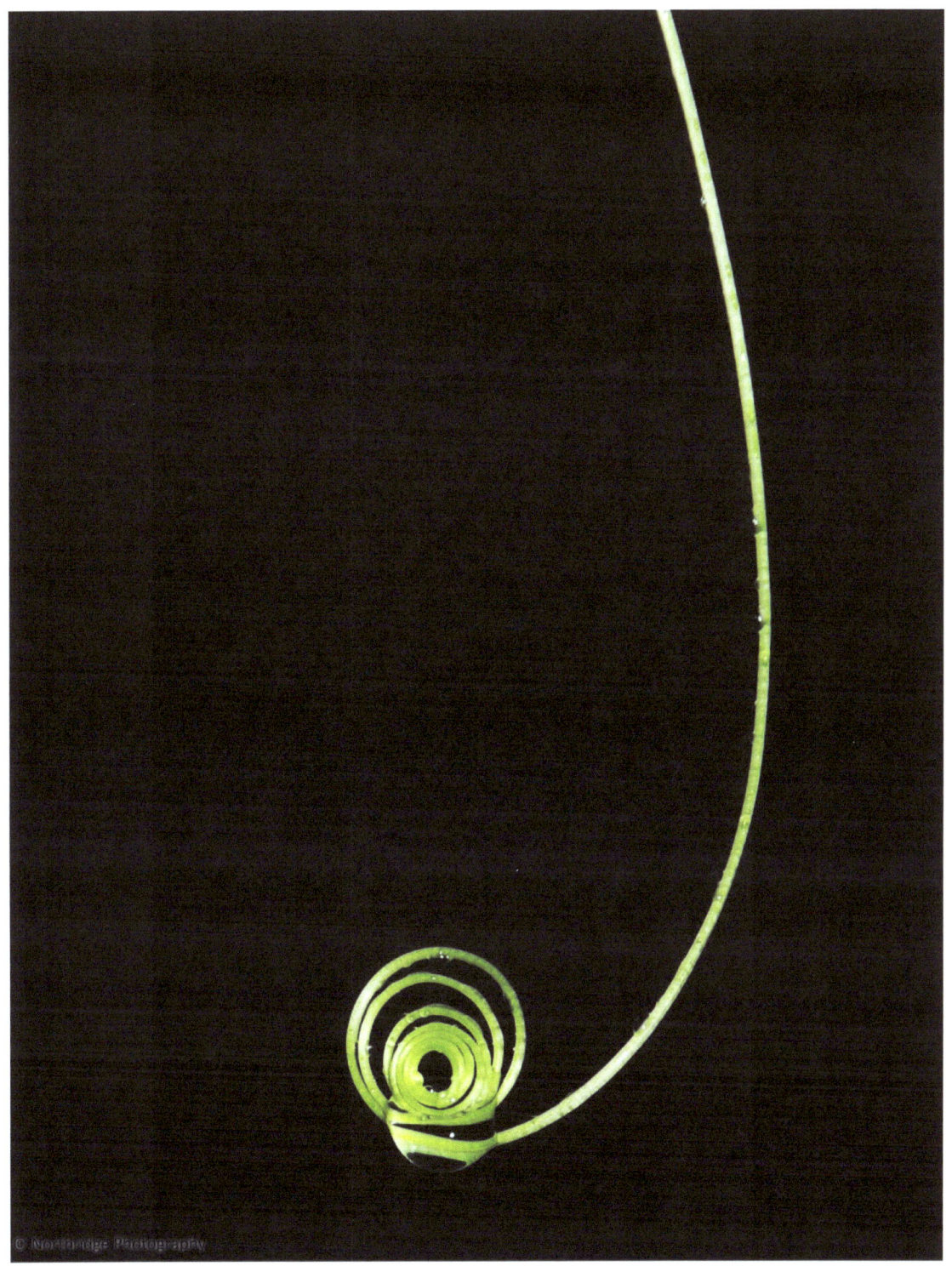

Captured

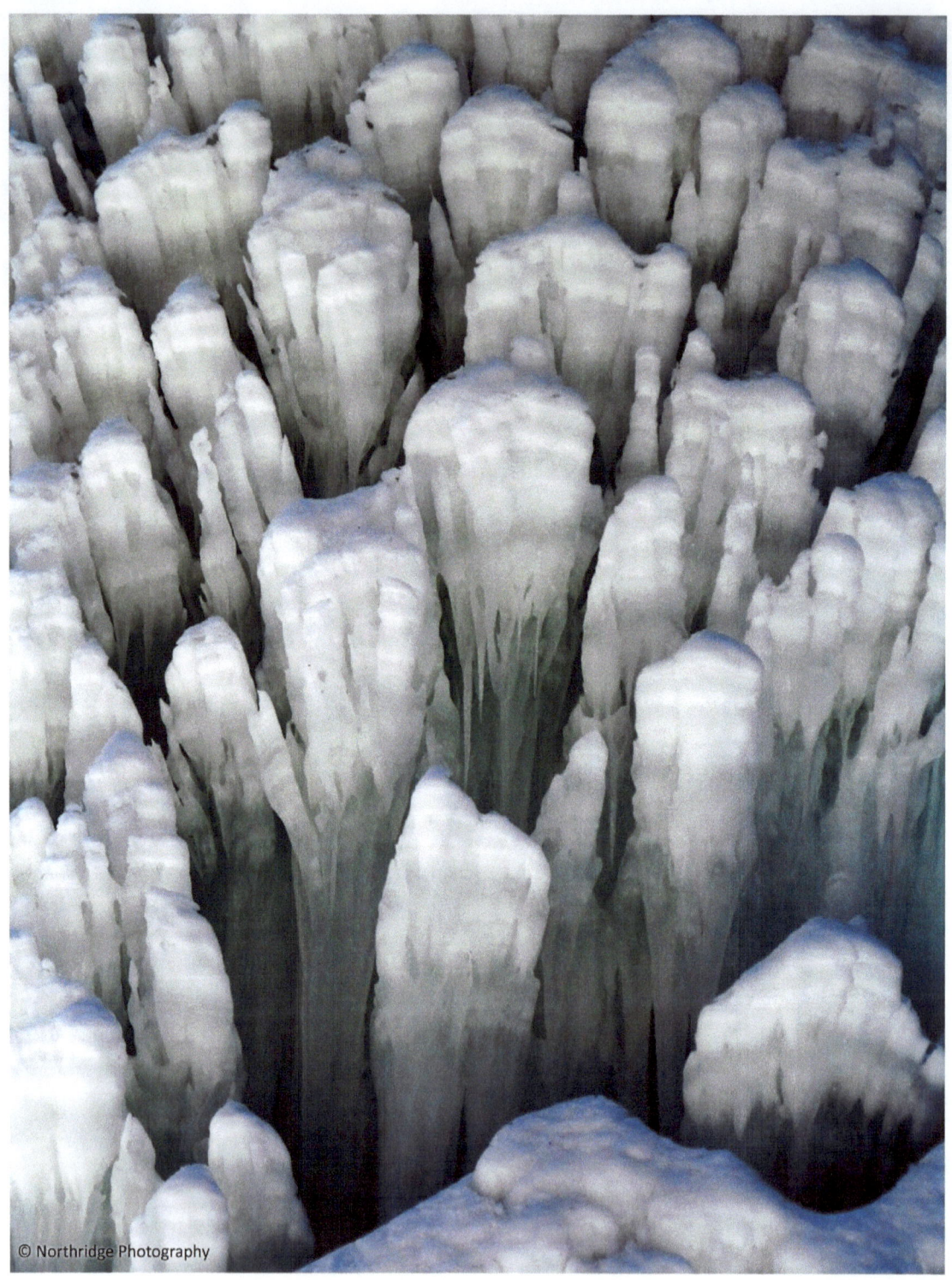

February

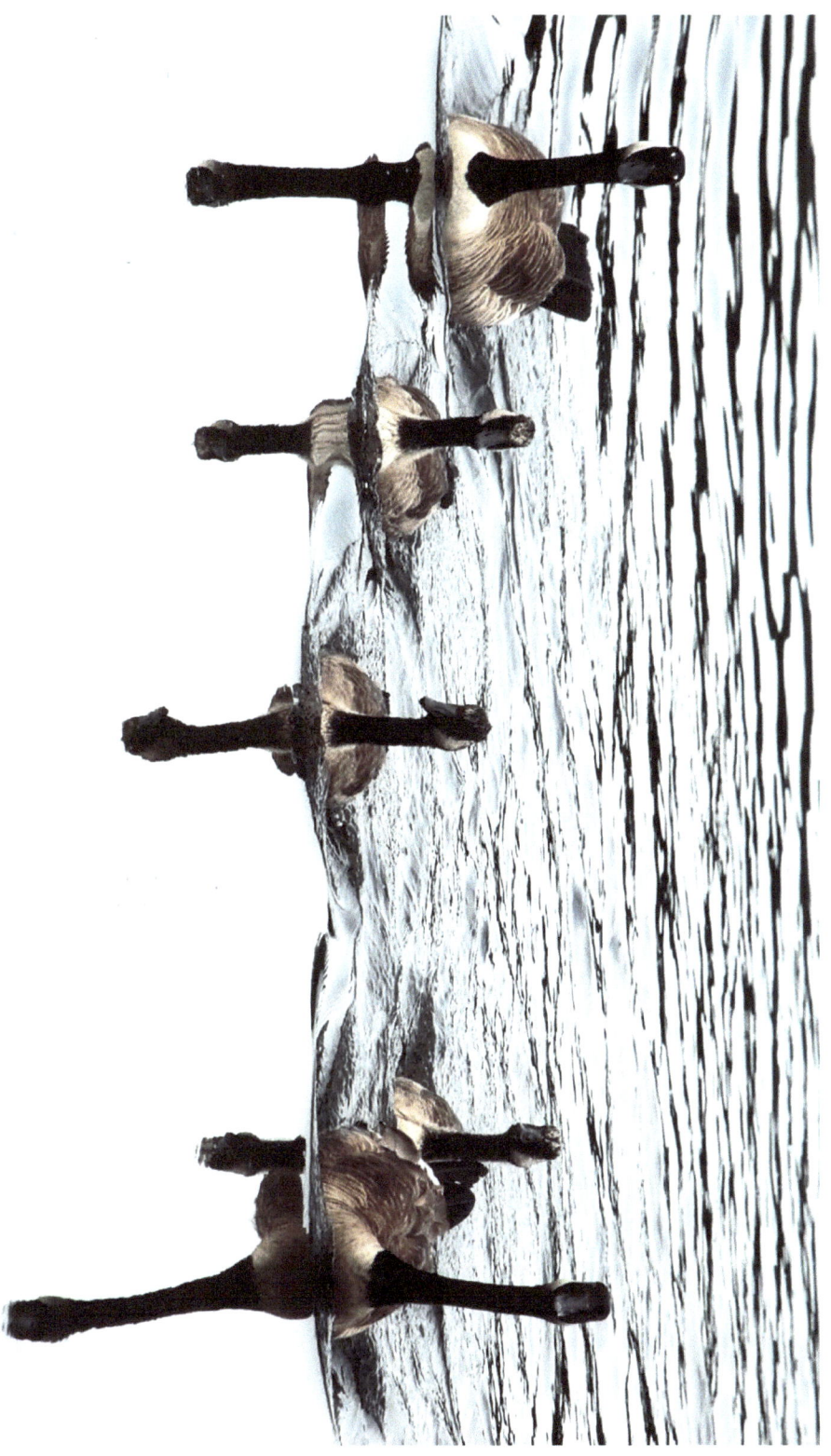

Canada Geese at Moss Lake

© Northridge Photography

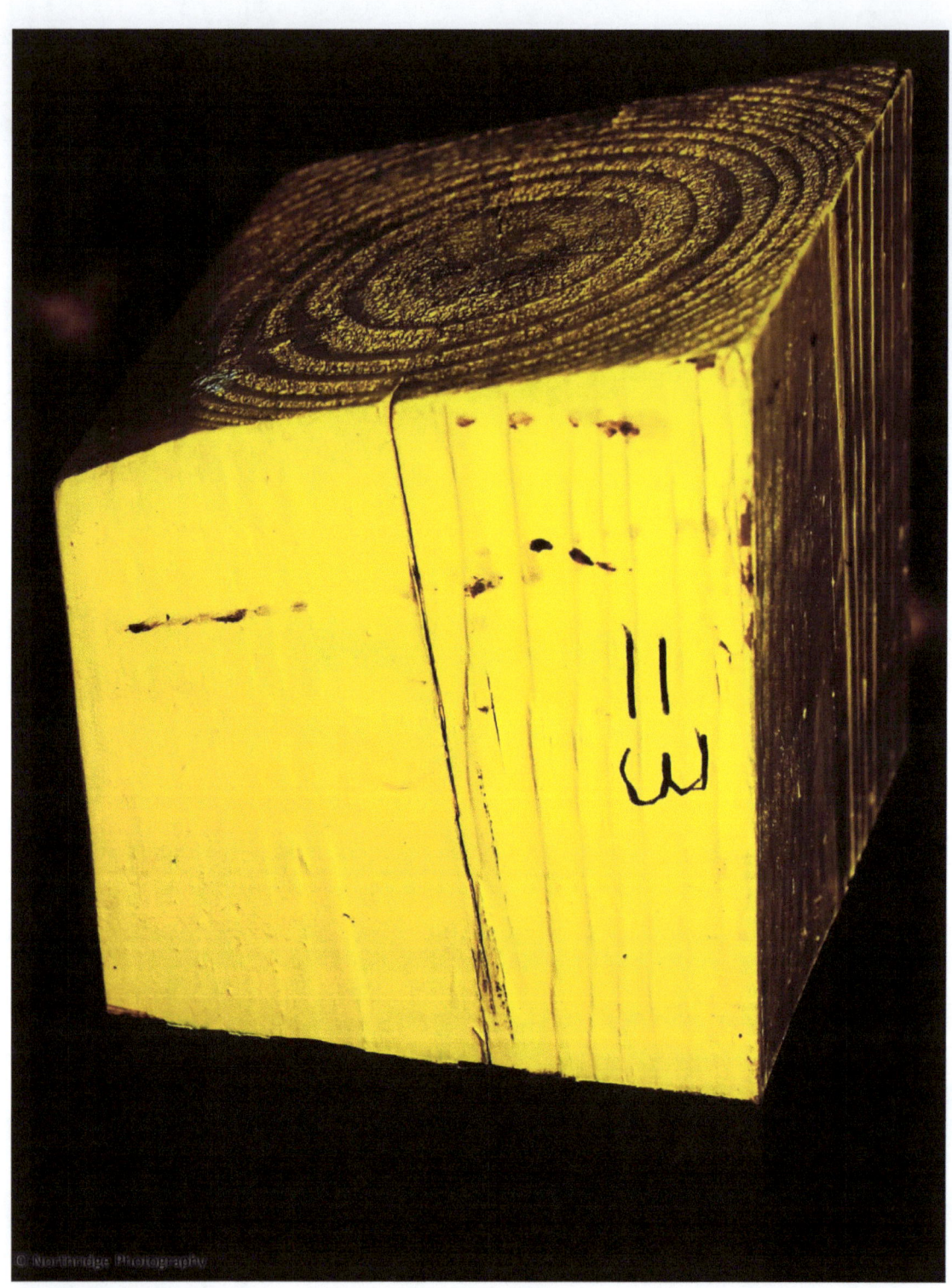

Scratching Post

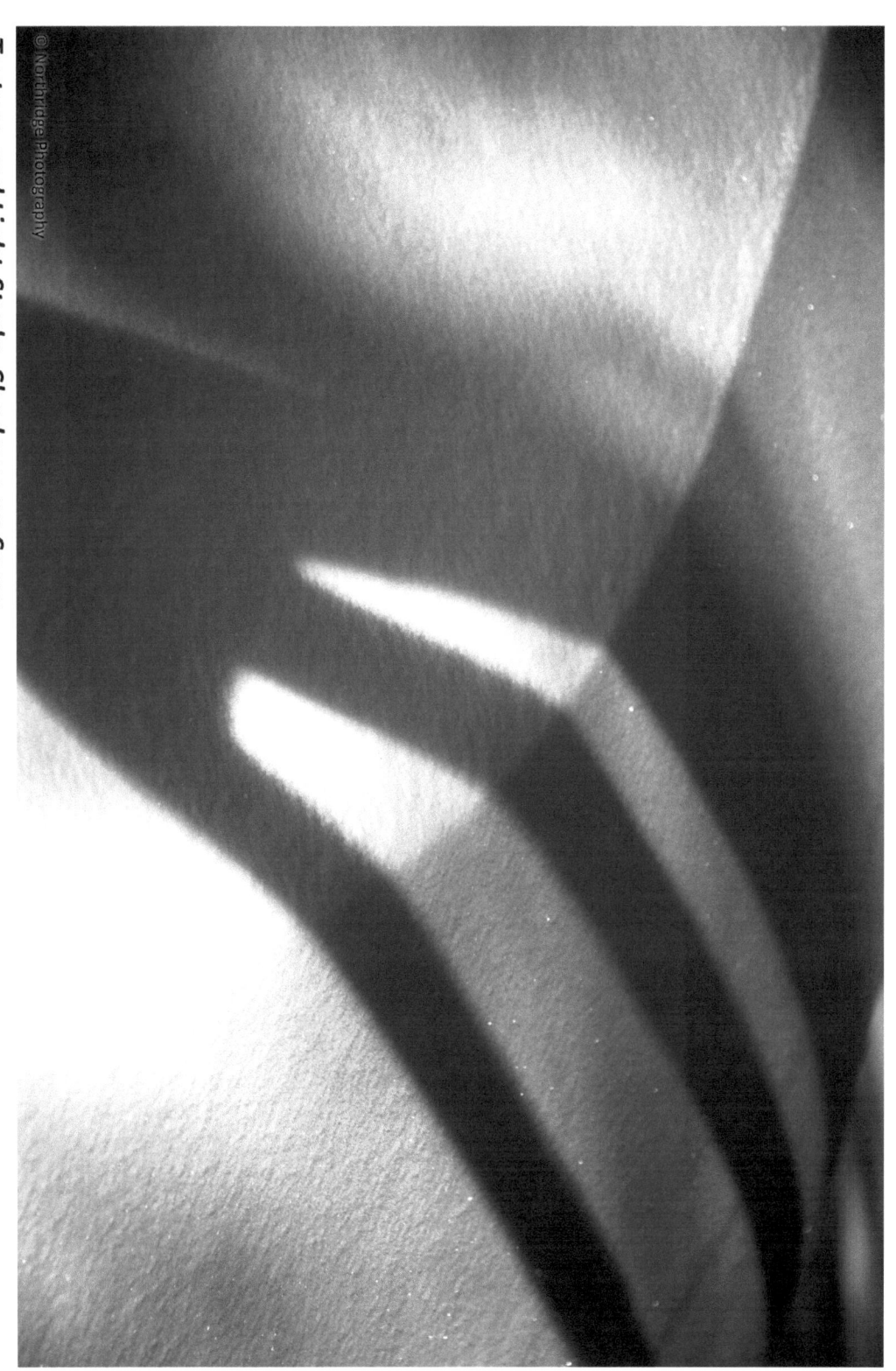

Texture and Light-Study; Shadows on Snow

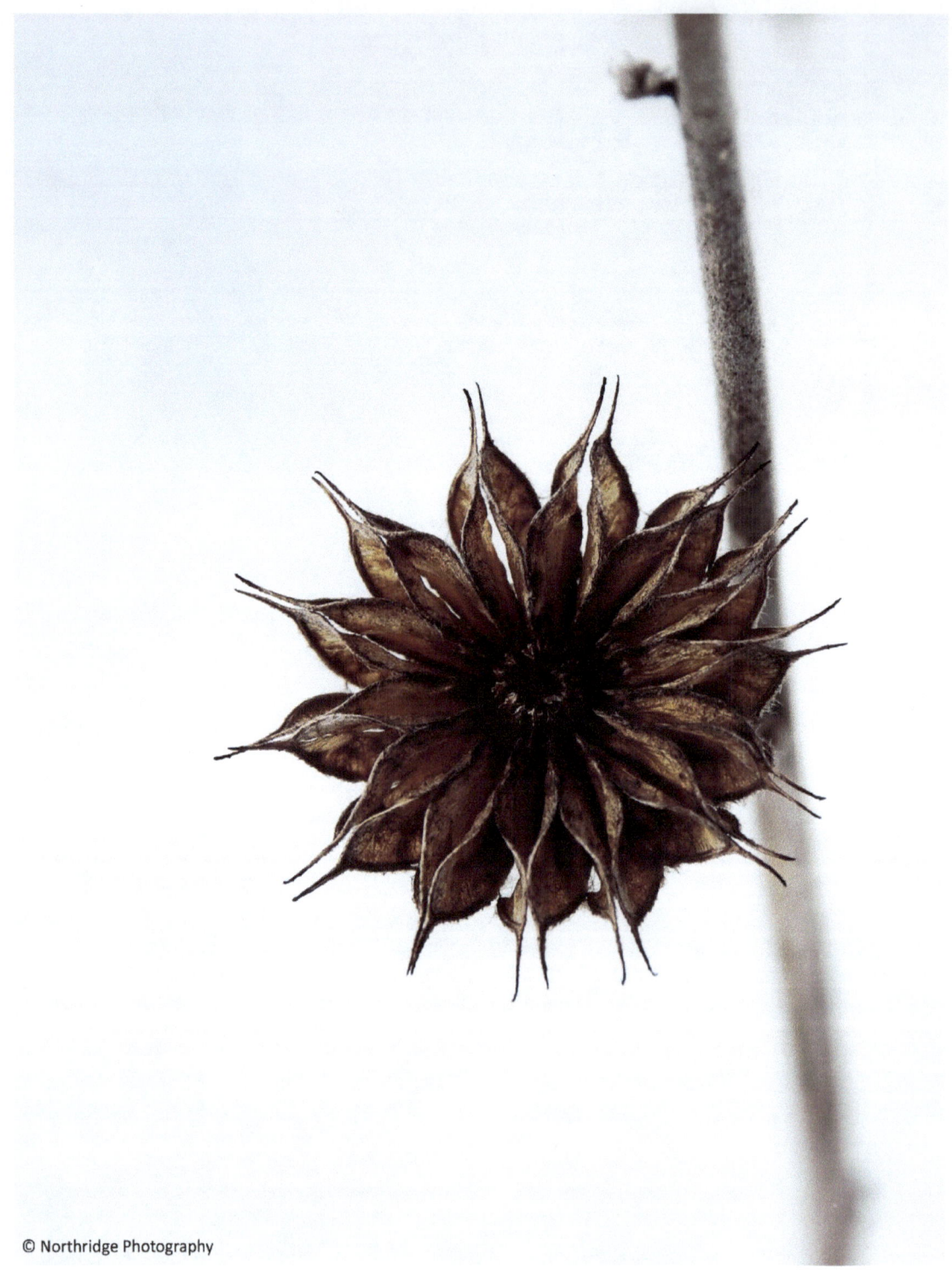

© Northridge Photography

In Winter

Sycamore © Northridge Photography

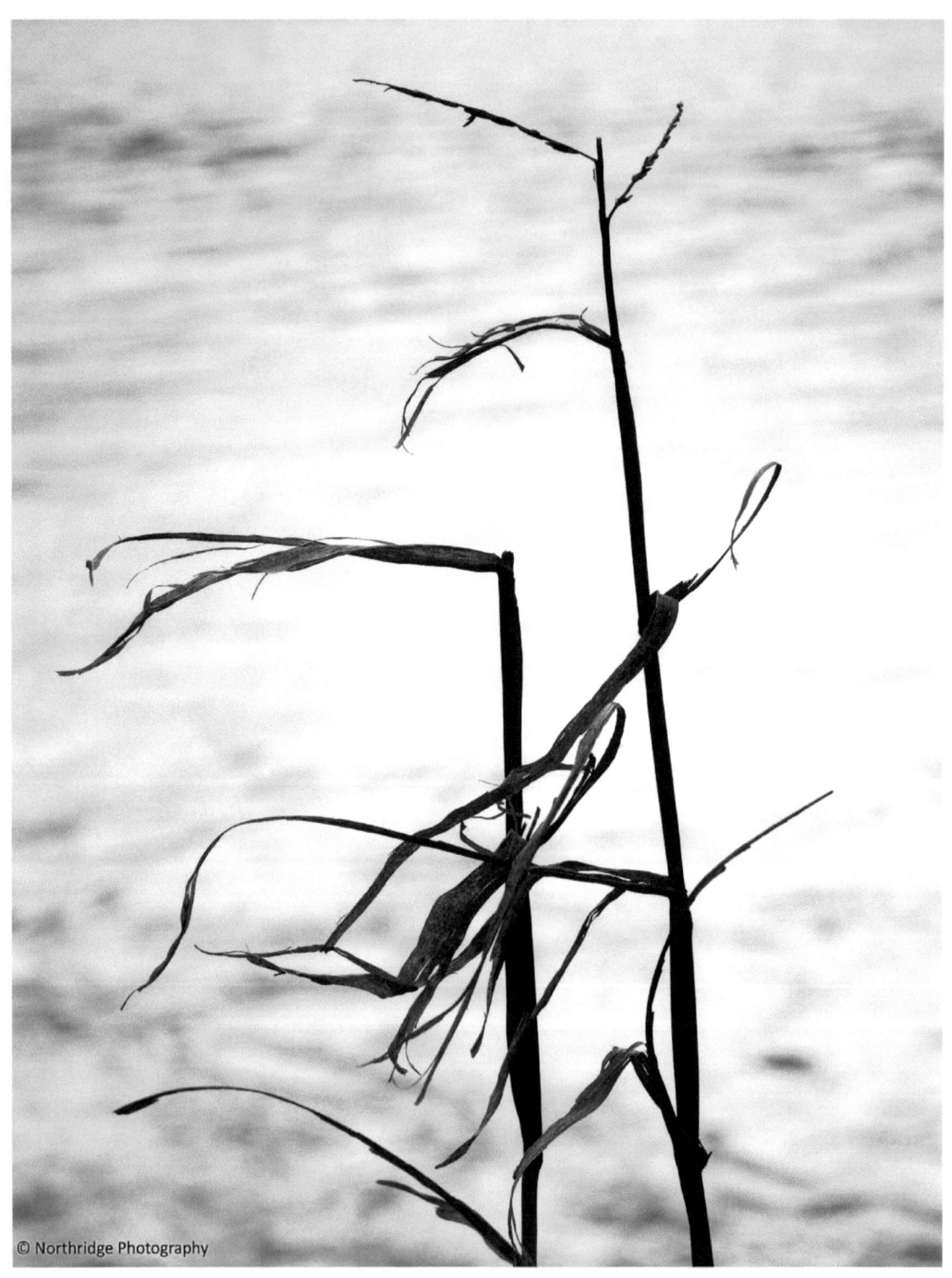

How do You Figure?

Drying Up © Northridge Photography

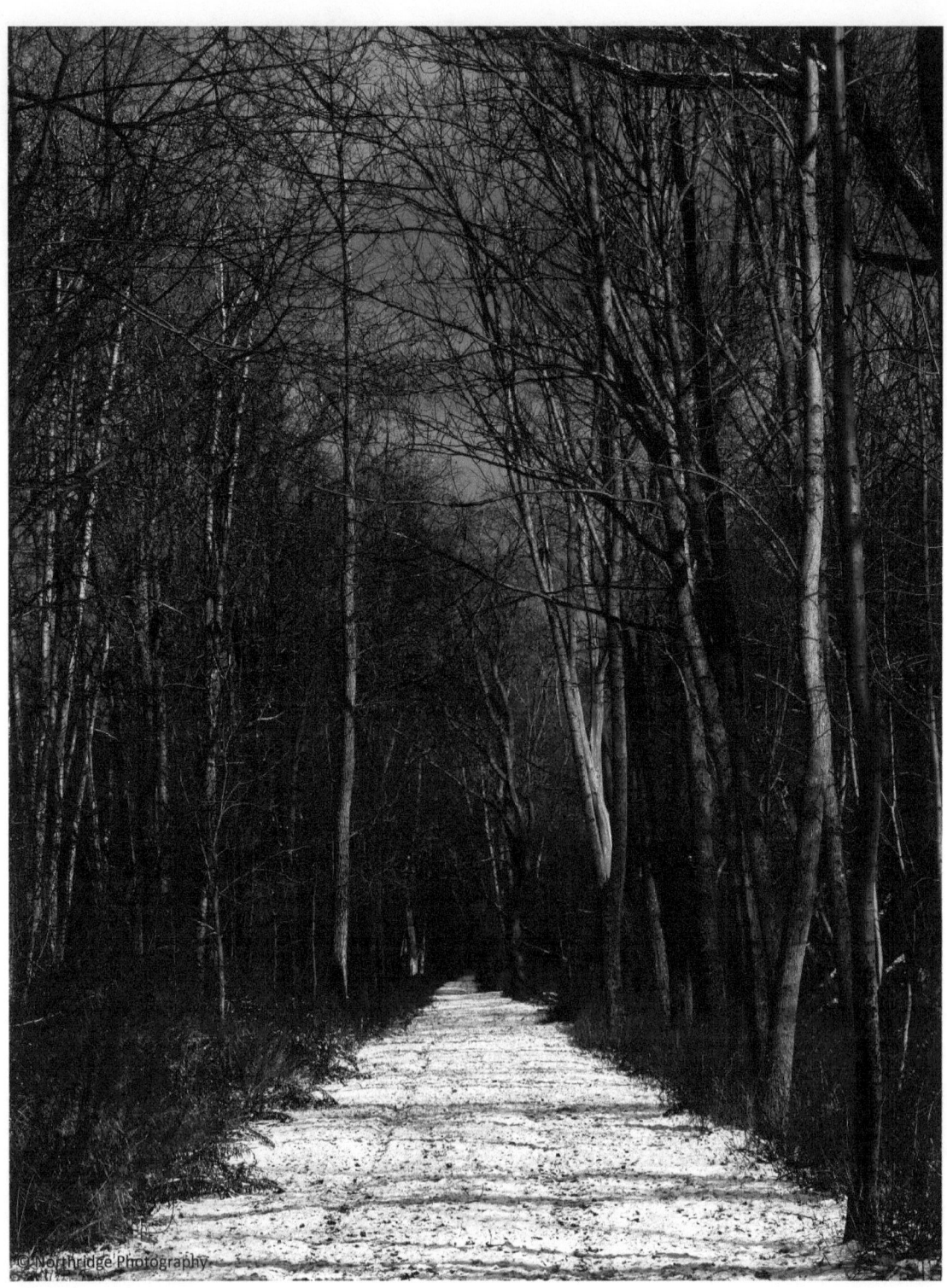
That's the Way

The Memory Remains

© Northridge Photography

Starlings

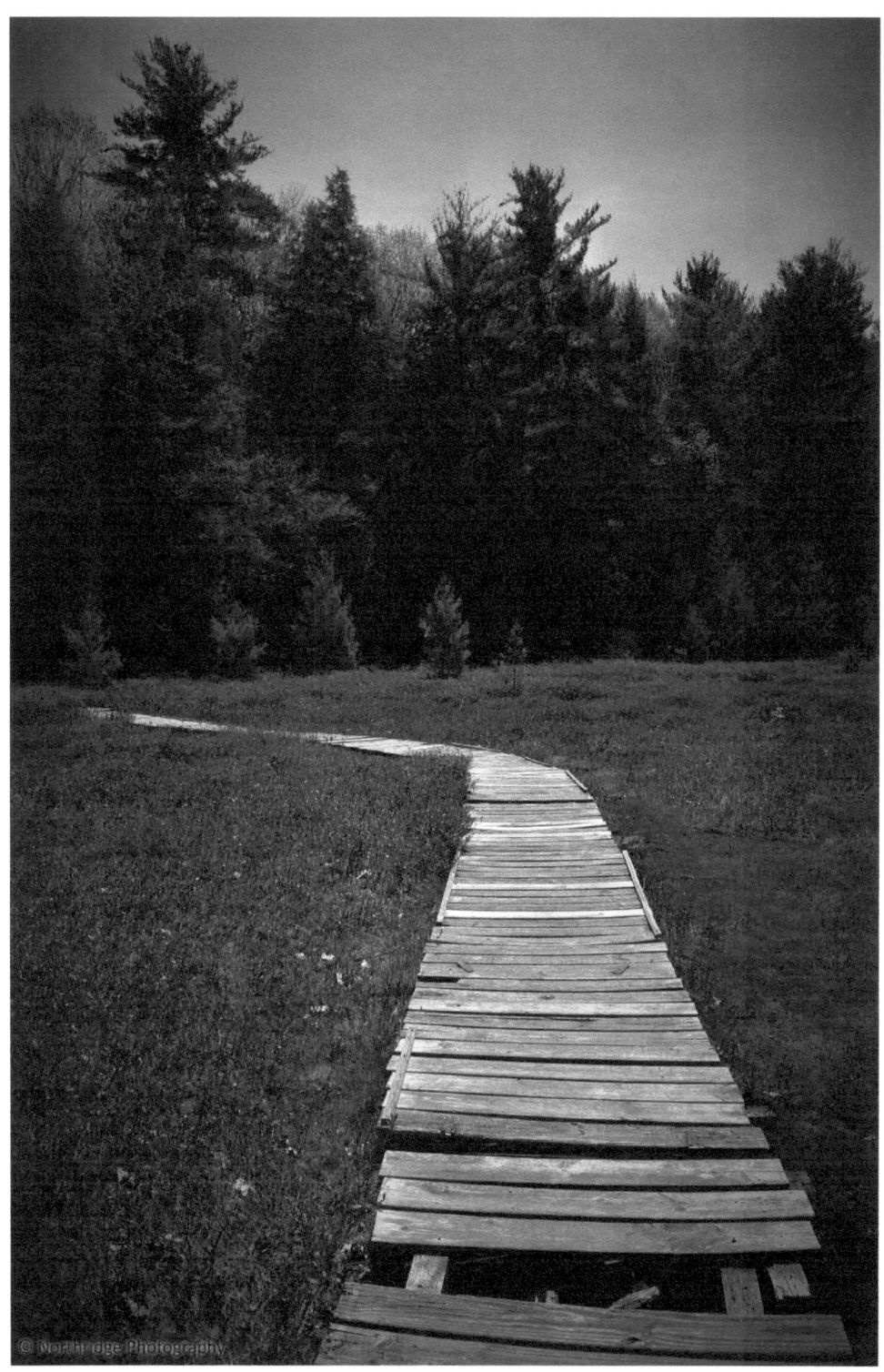

The Bog

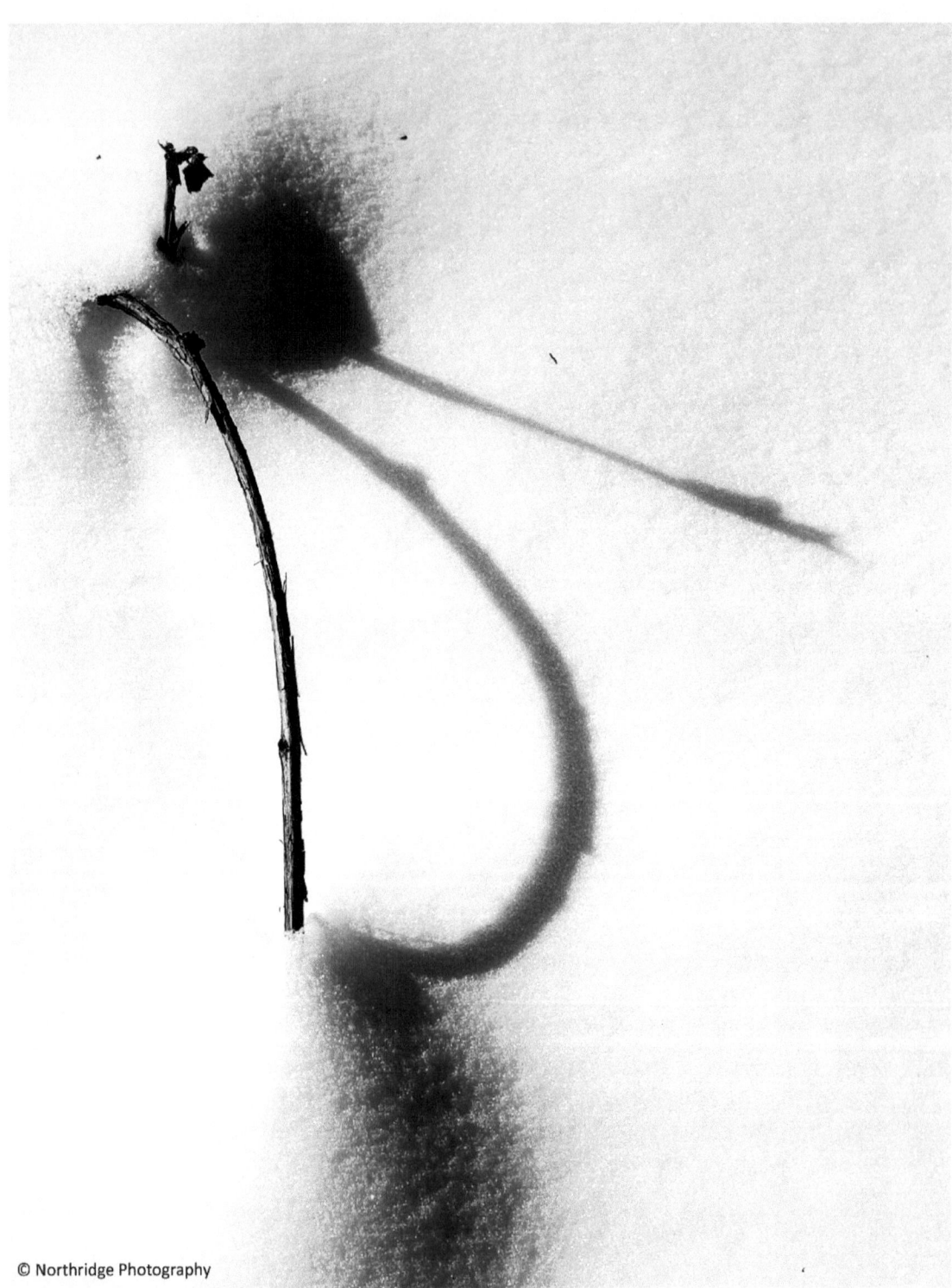

Hitchcock

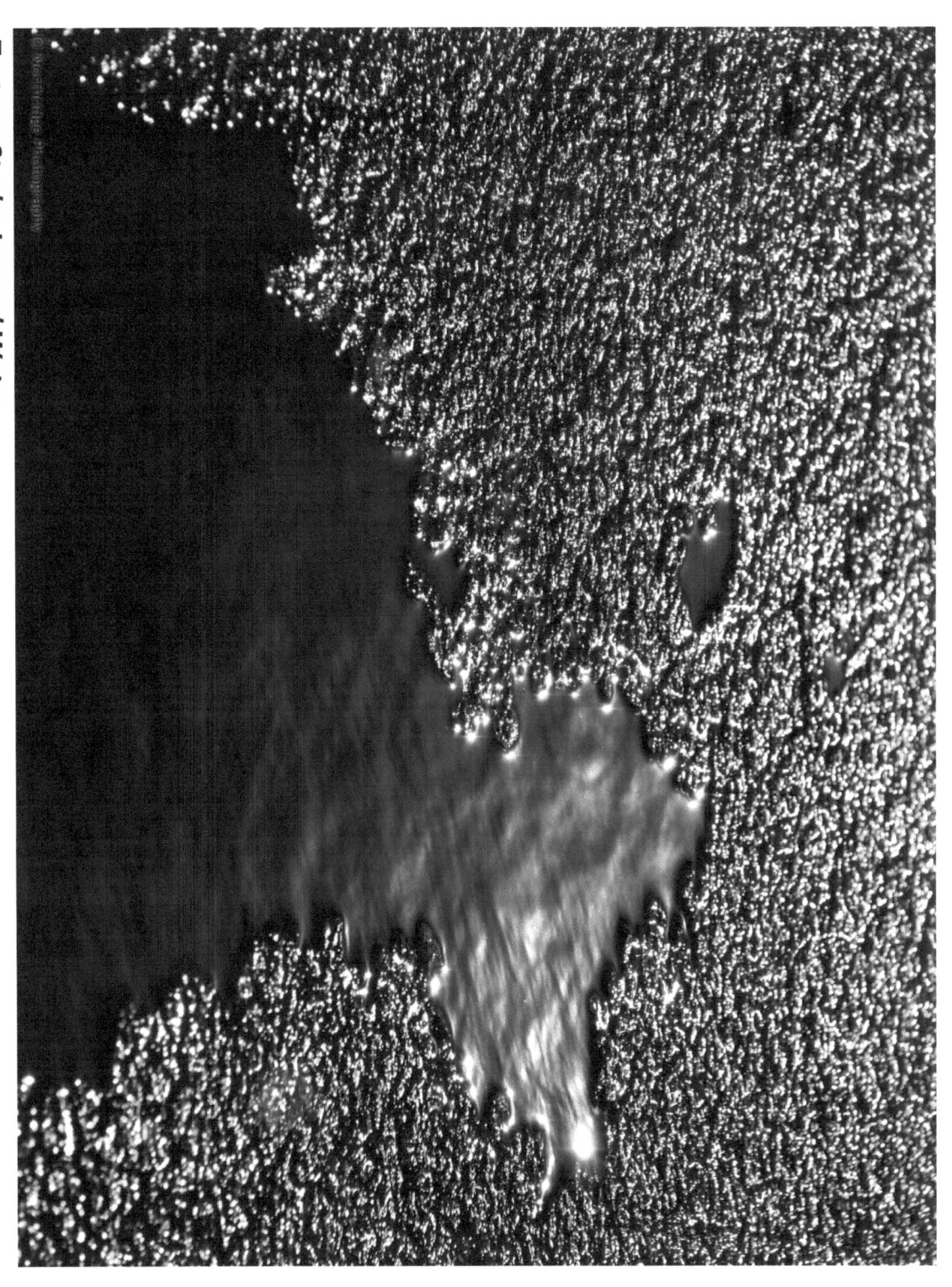

Texture-Study; Ice and Water

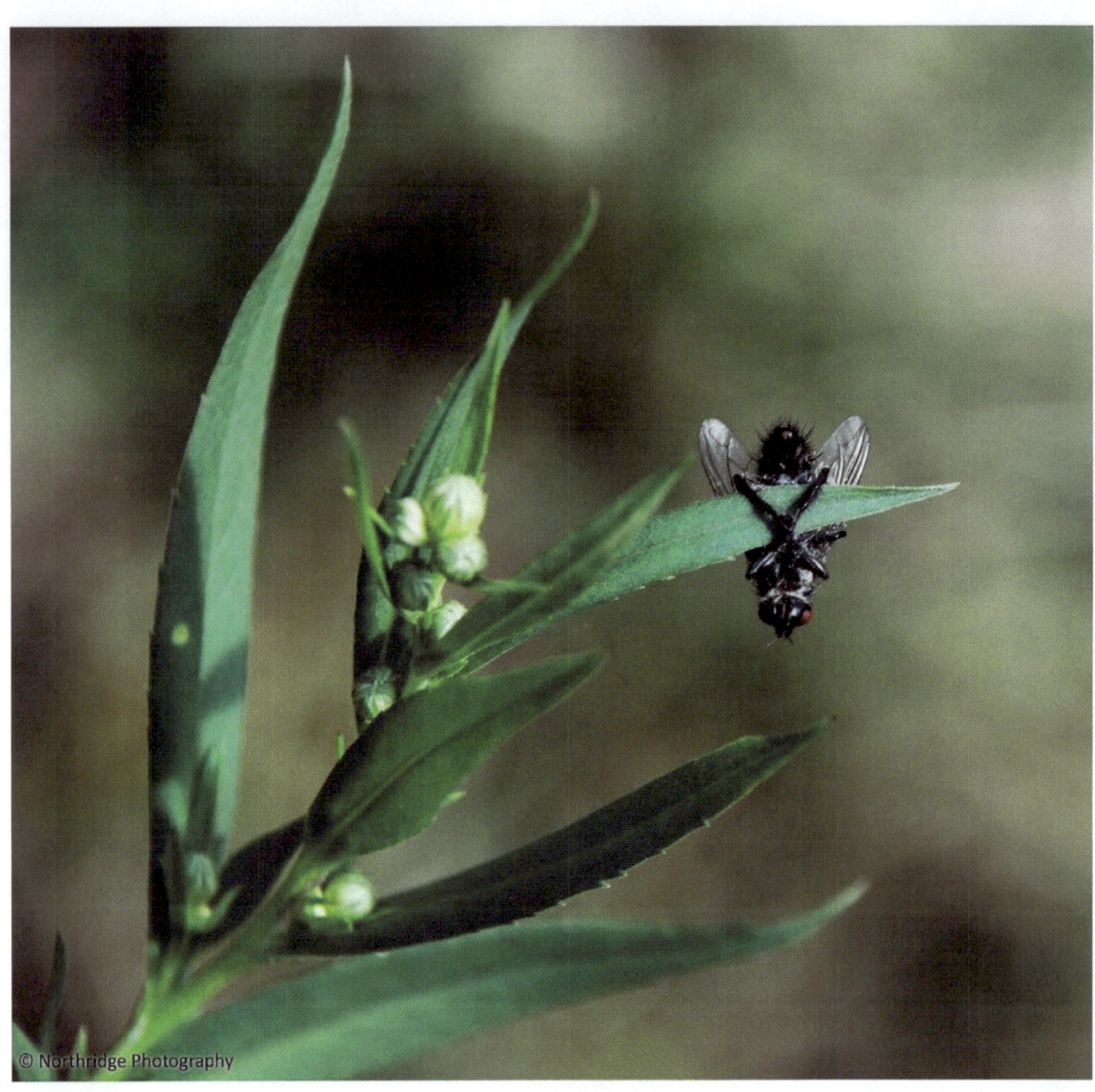

Insecure

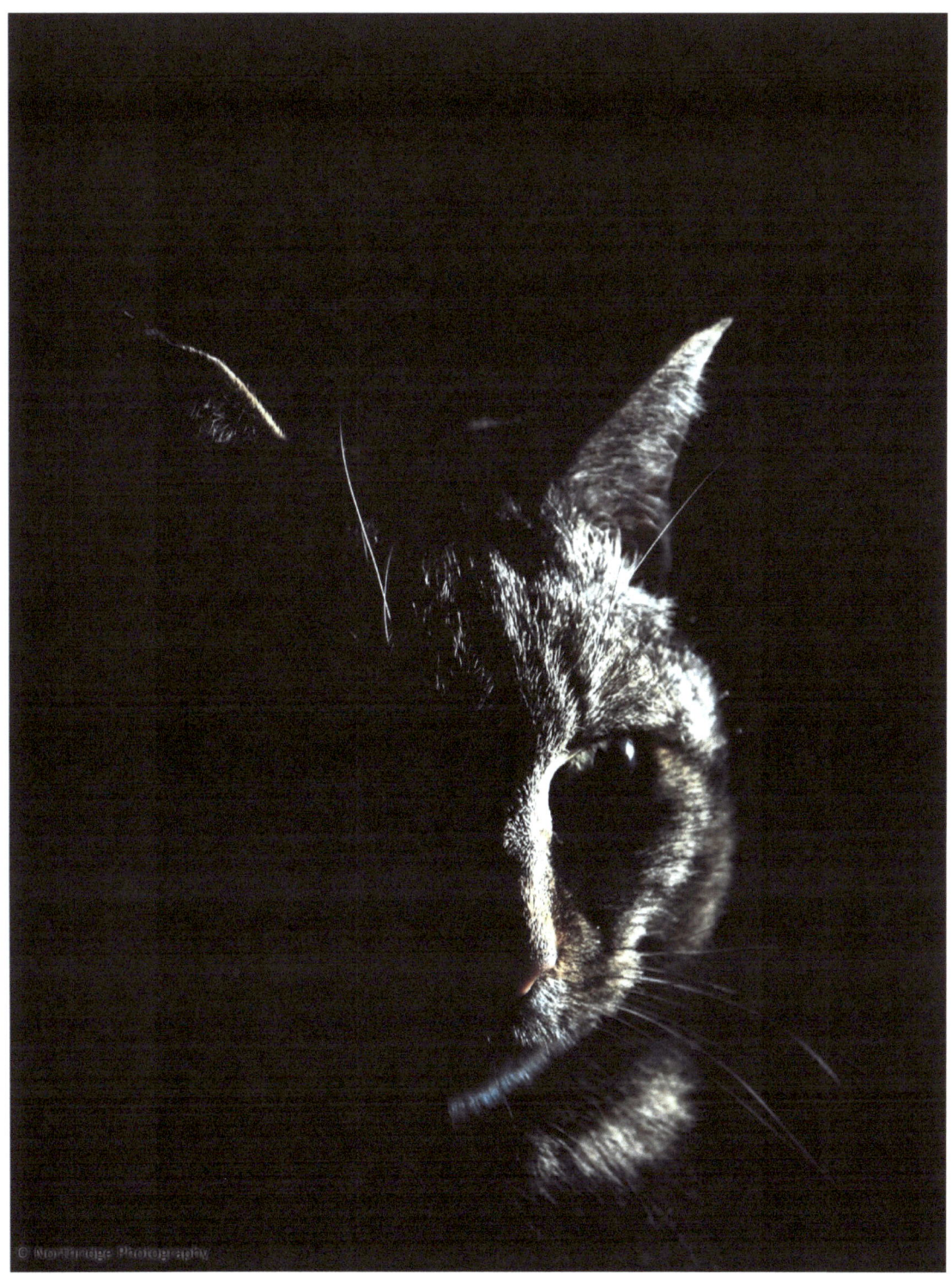

Light-Study

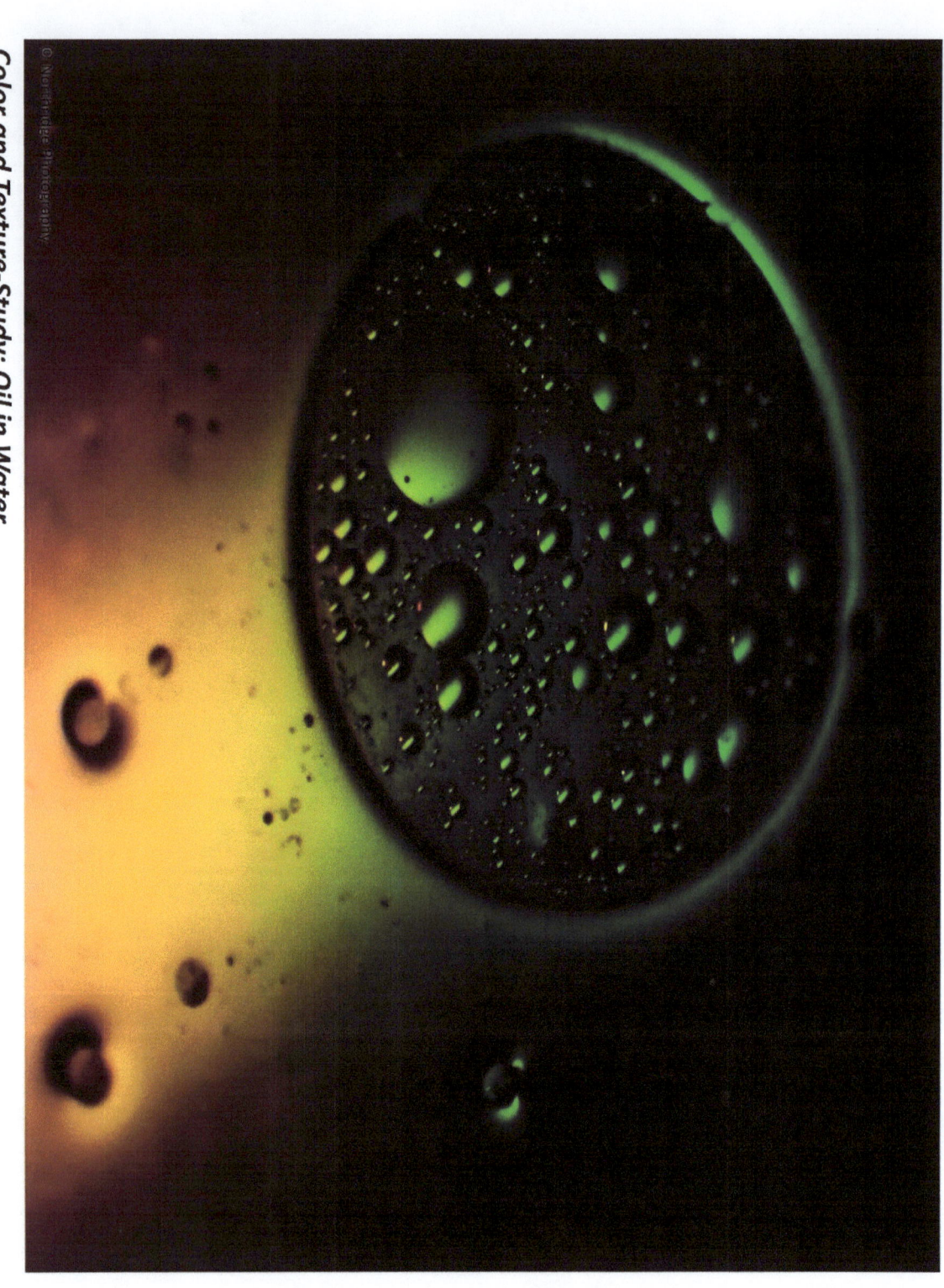

Color and Texture-Study; Oil in Water

Wetland

First Light

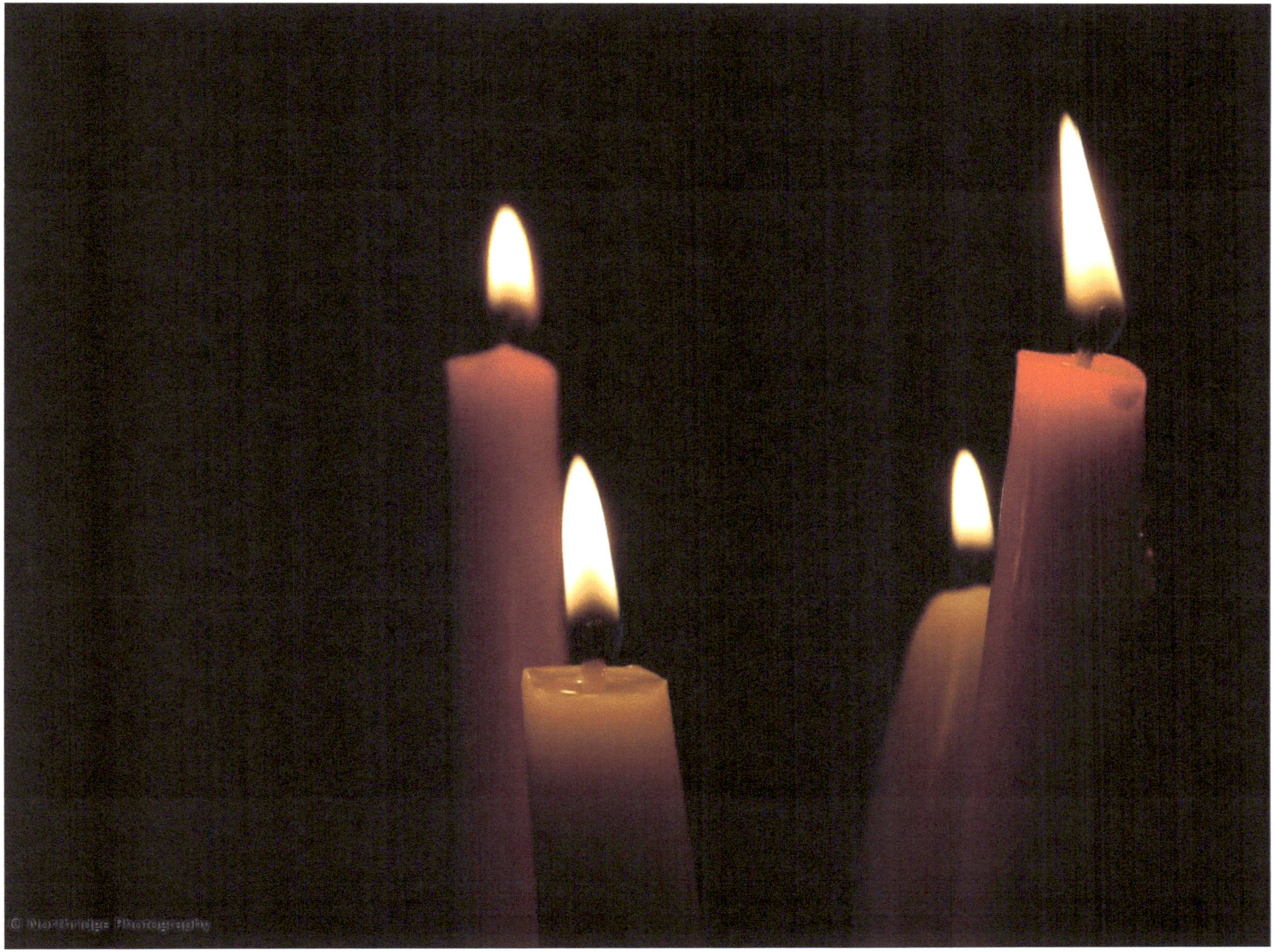

Catacombs

© NiaPartridge Photography

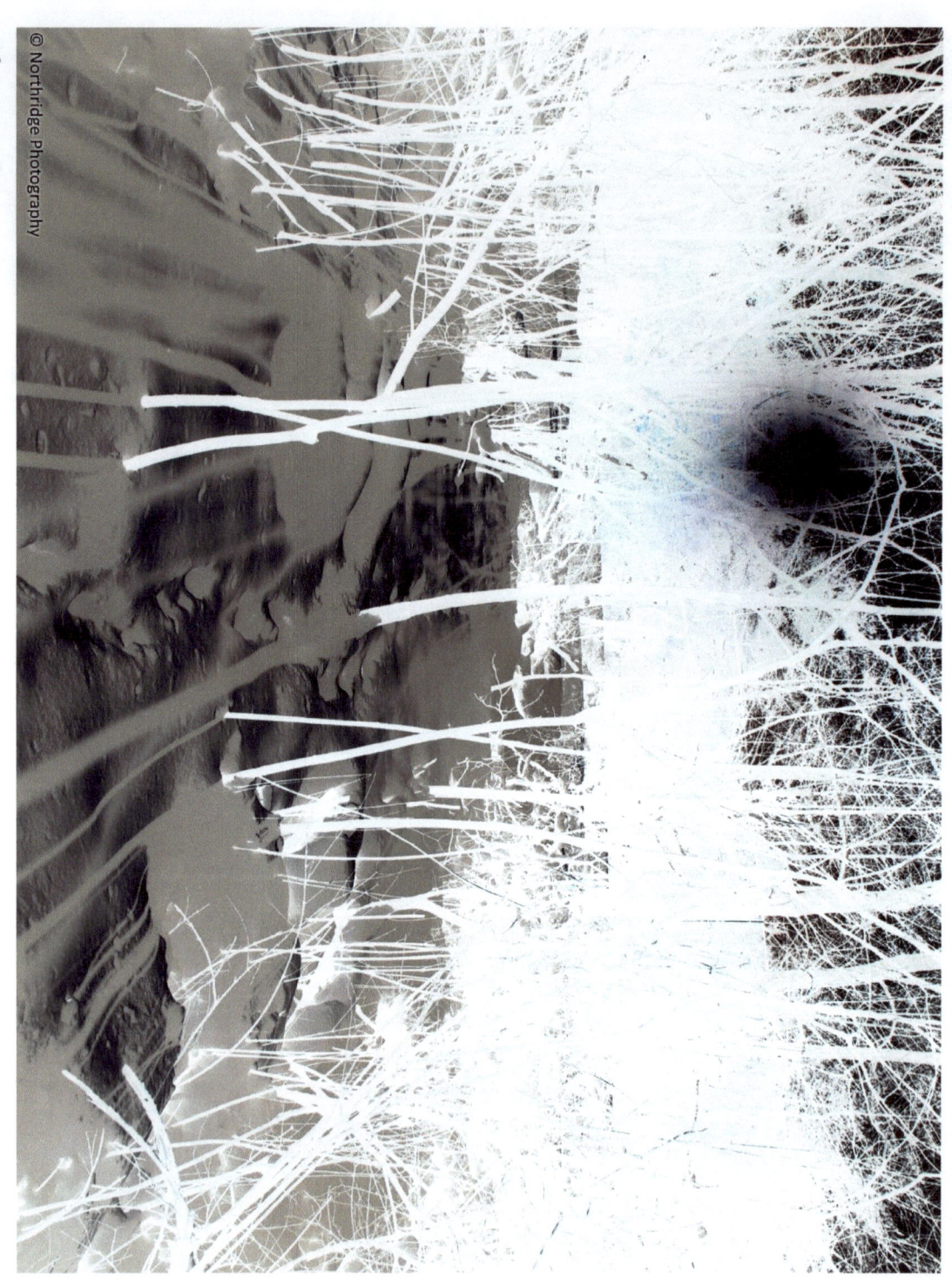

Abstract Sun — © Northridge Photography

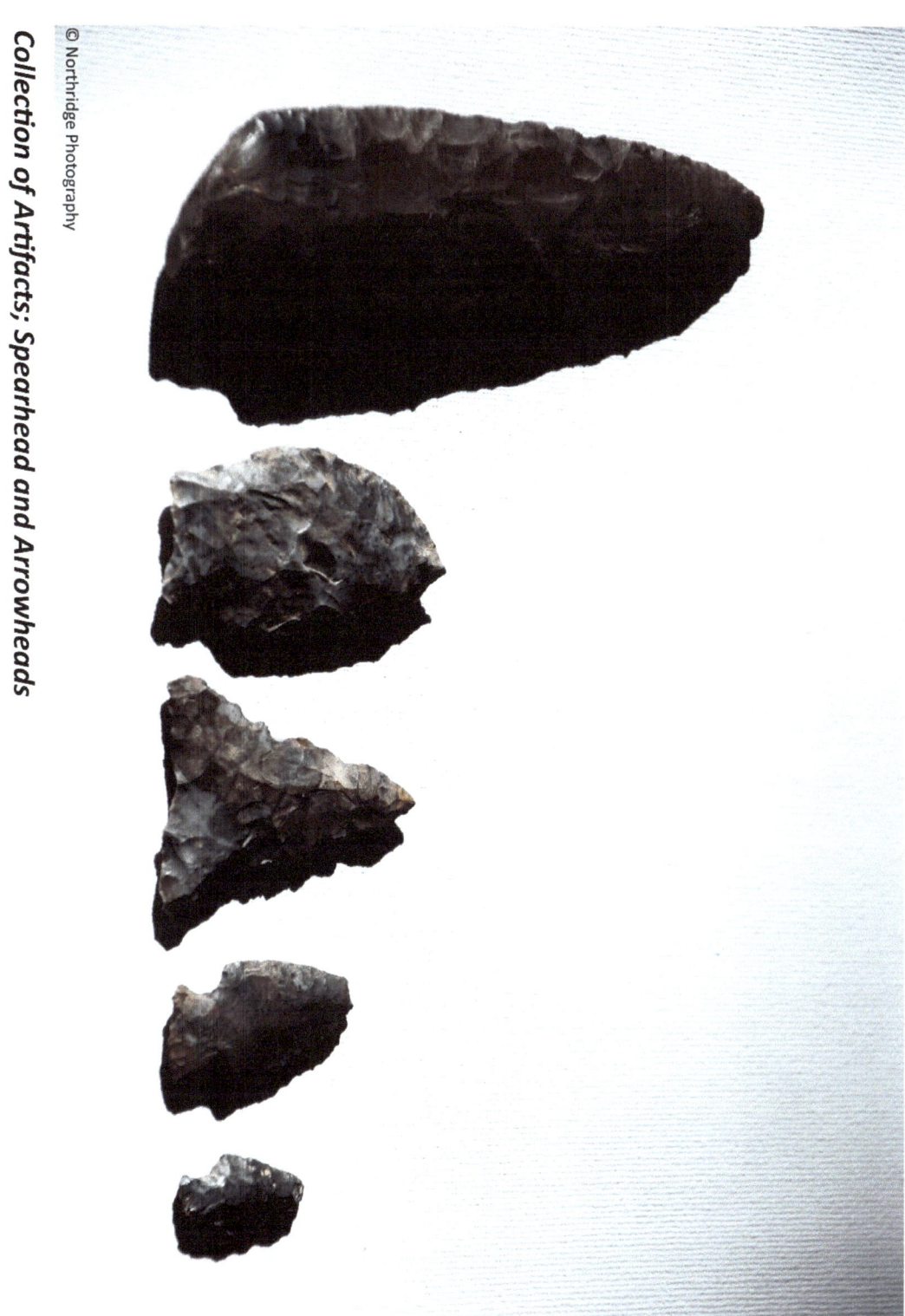

Collection of Artifacts; Spearhead and Arrowheads
© Northridge Photography

Knickknack

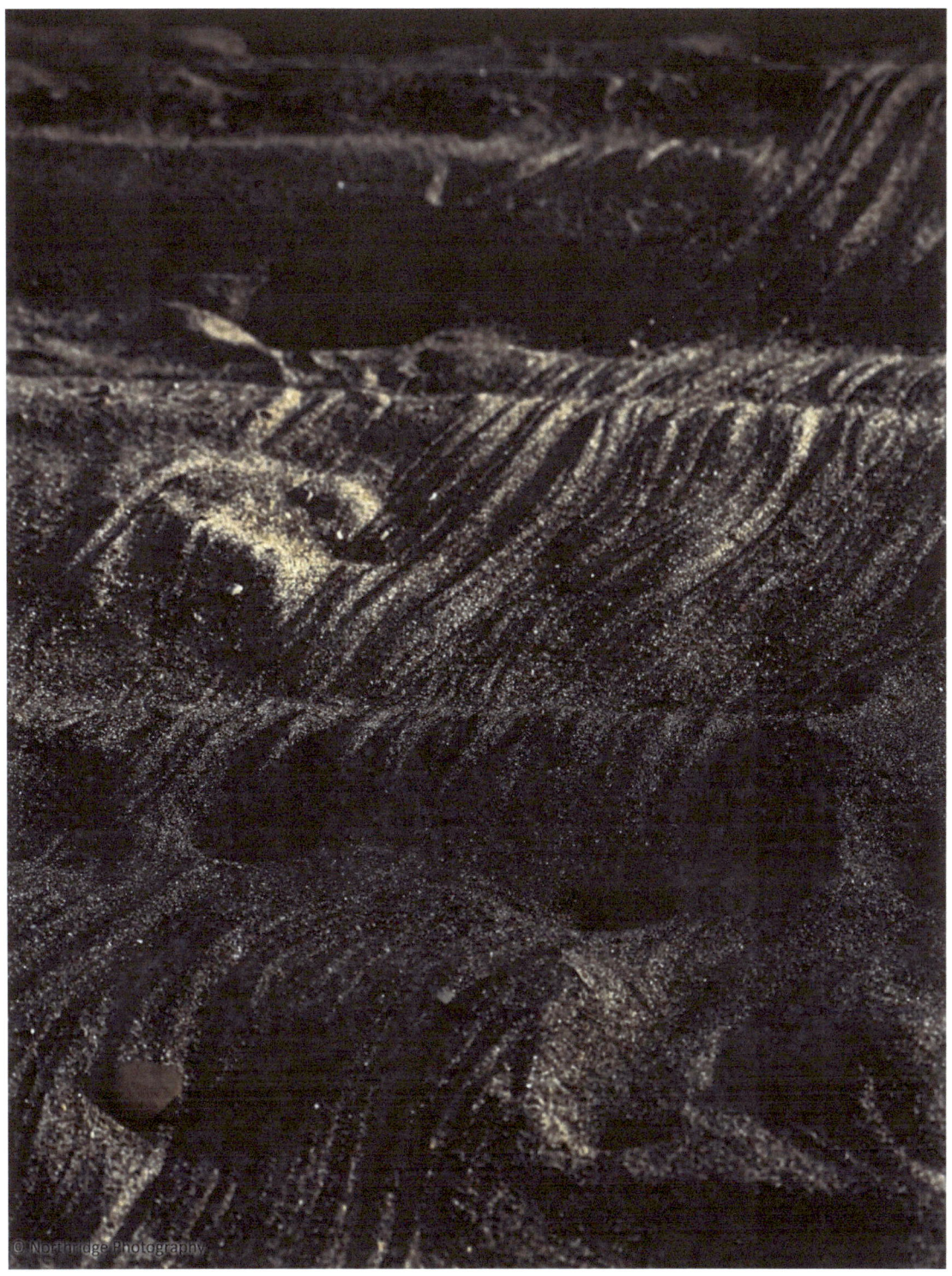

Zen on the Beach

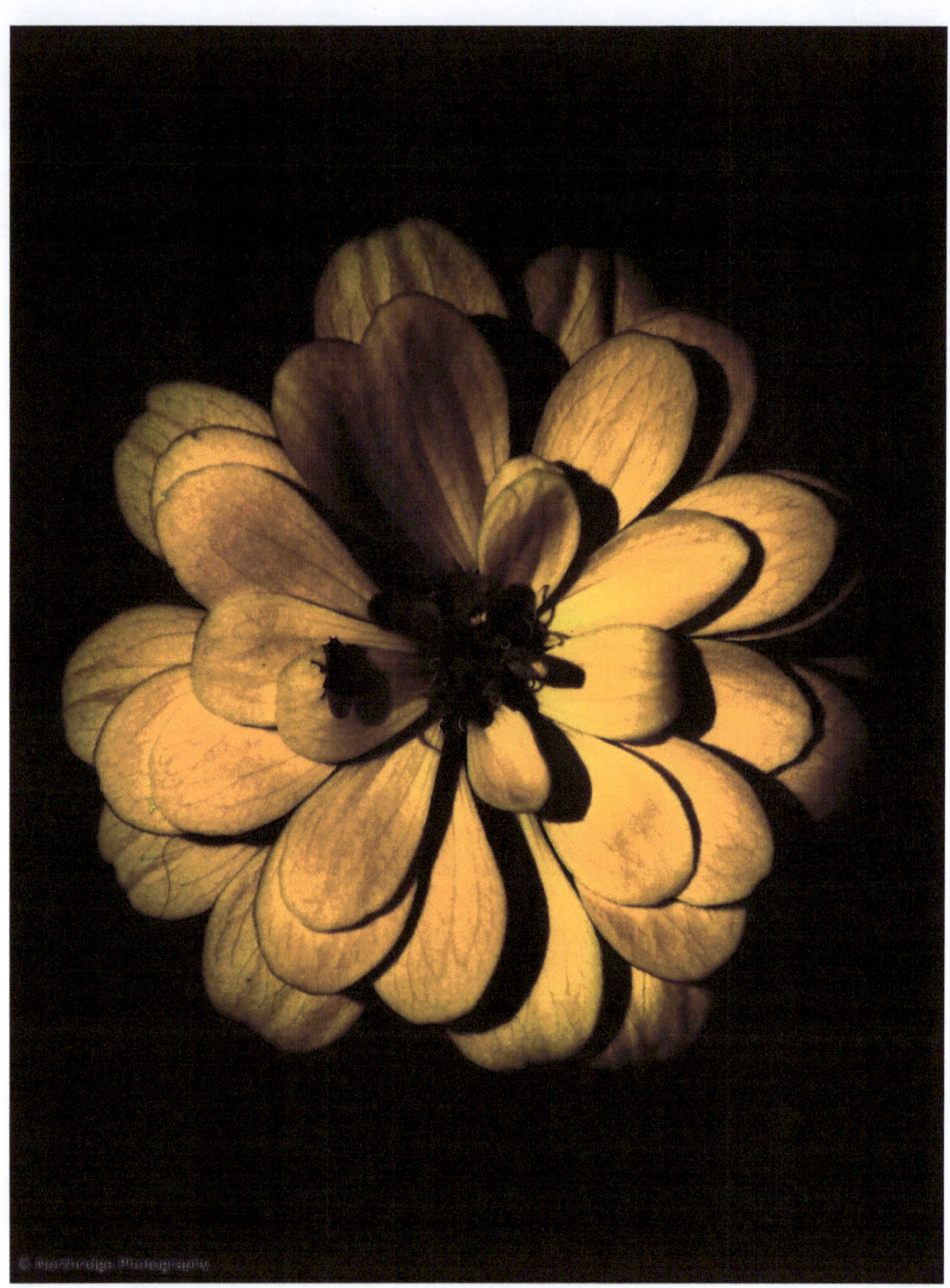

Fly on Yellow

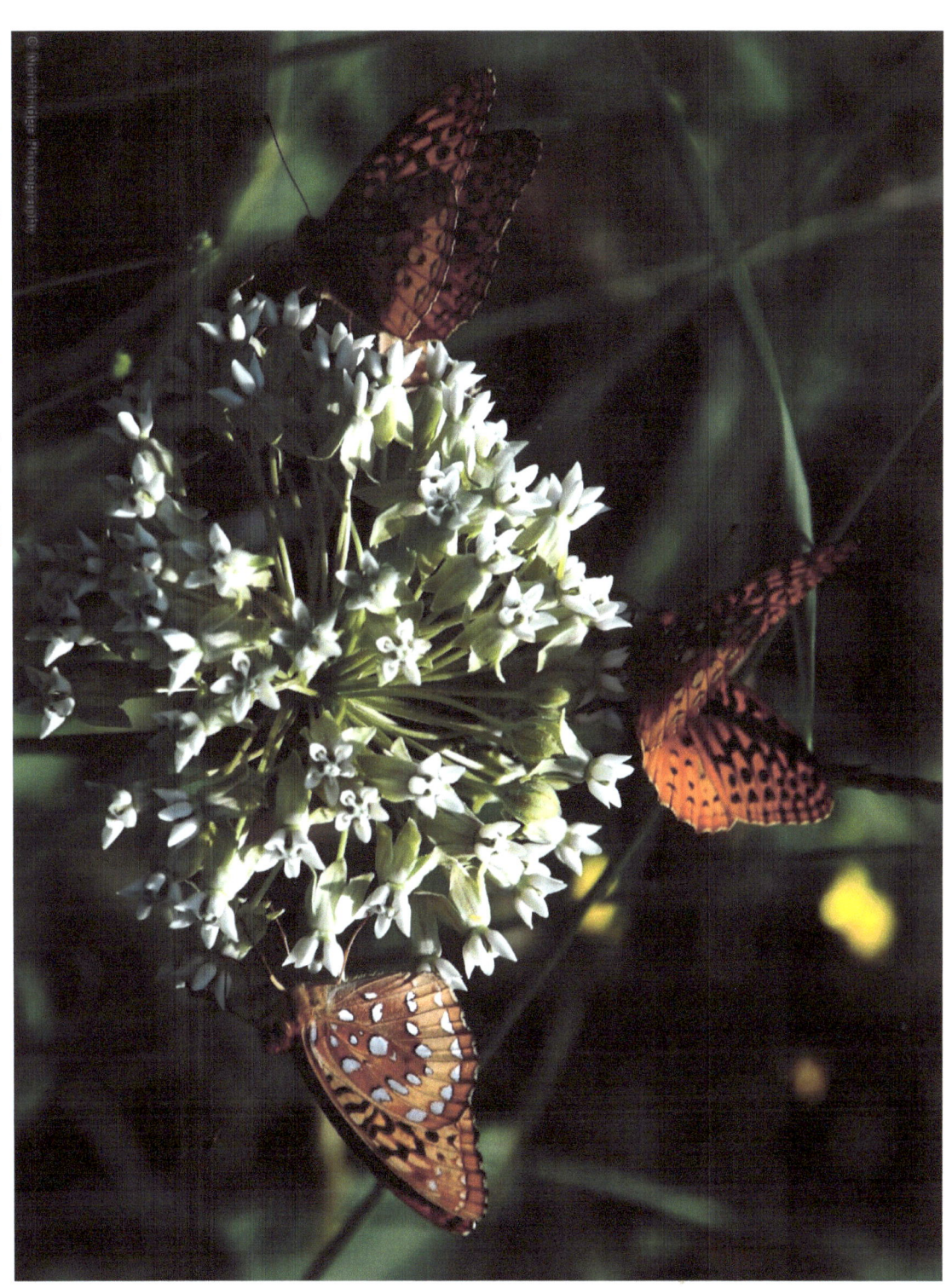

Three Butterflies; Great-Spangled Fritillary

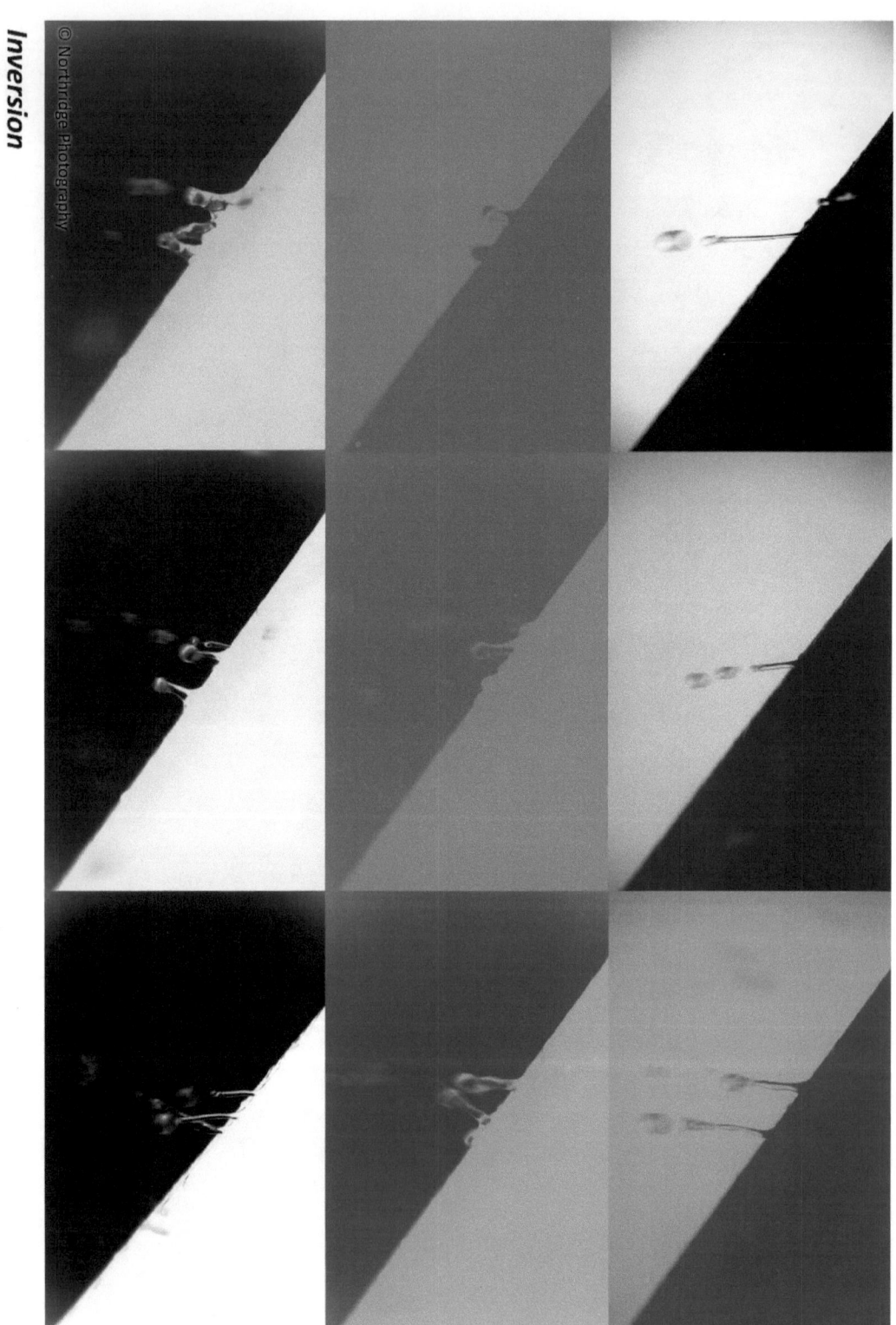

Inversion © Northridge Photography

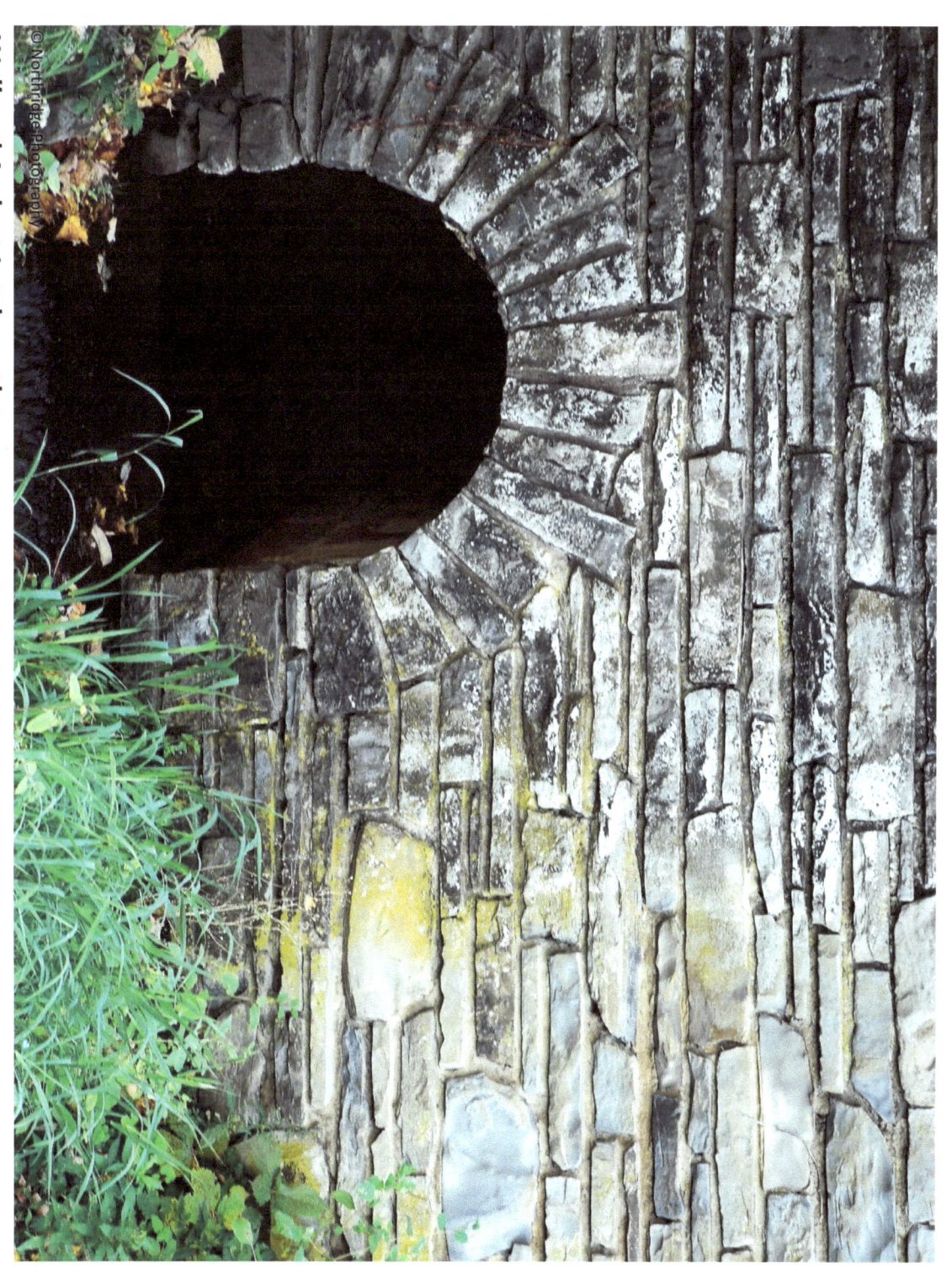
Wall and Arch at Letchworth

Winter Wonderland

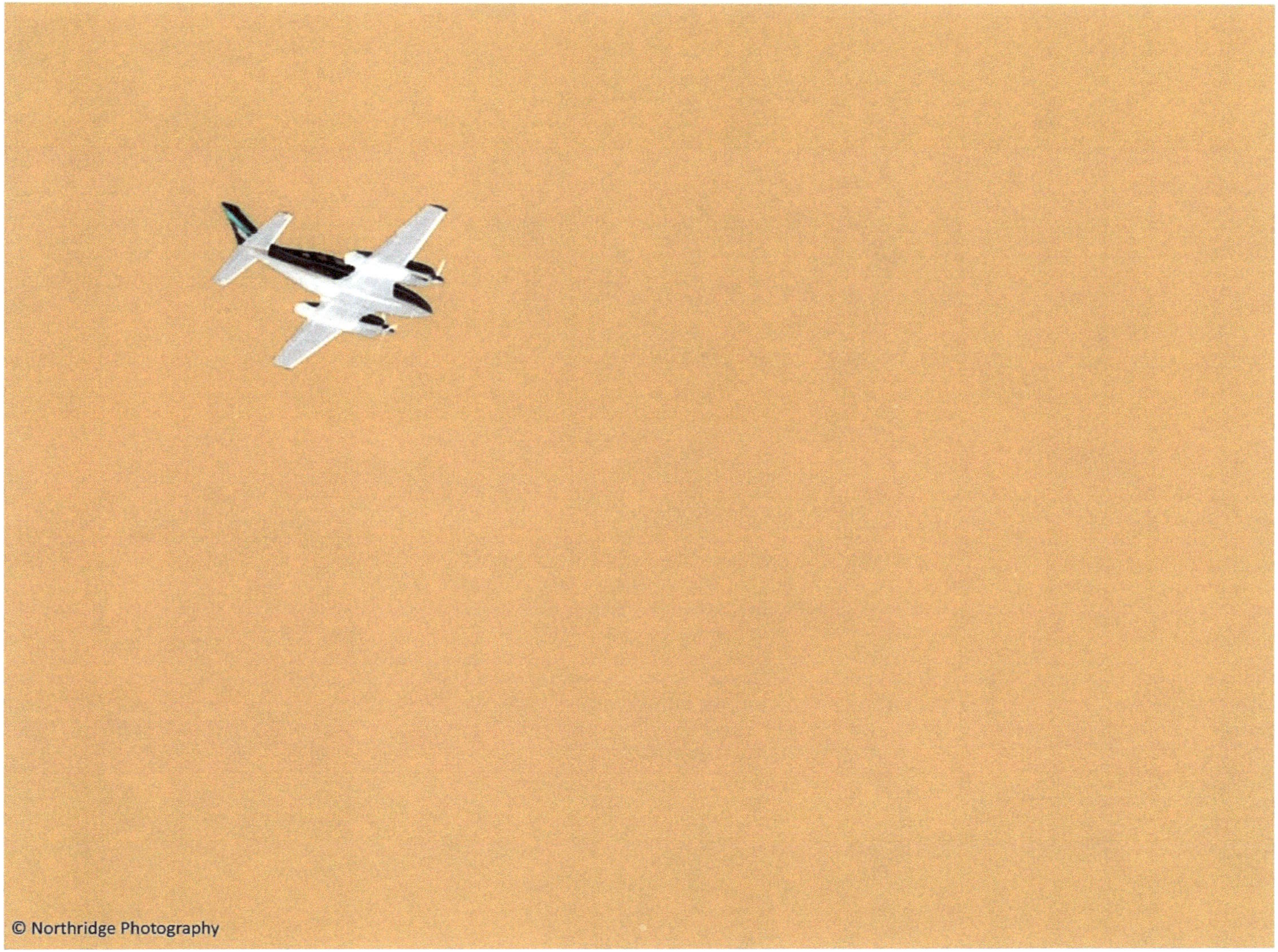

On a Plane

© Northridge Photography

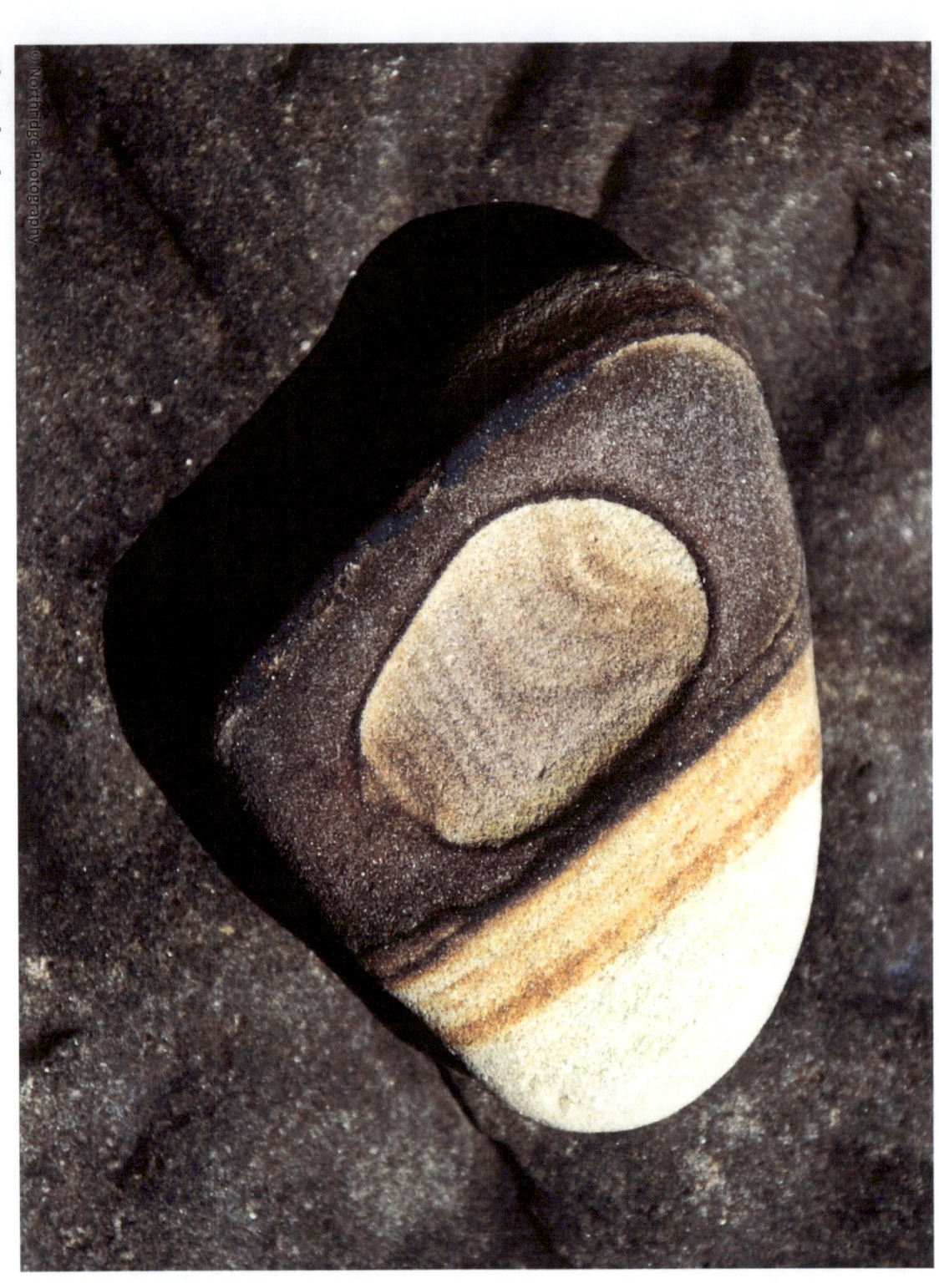

Thumbprint

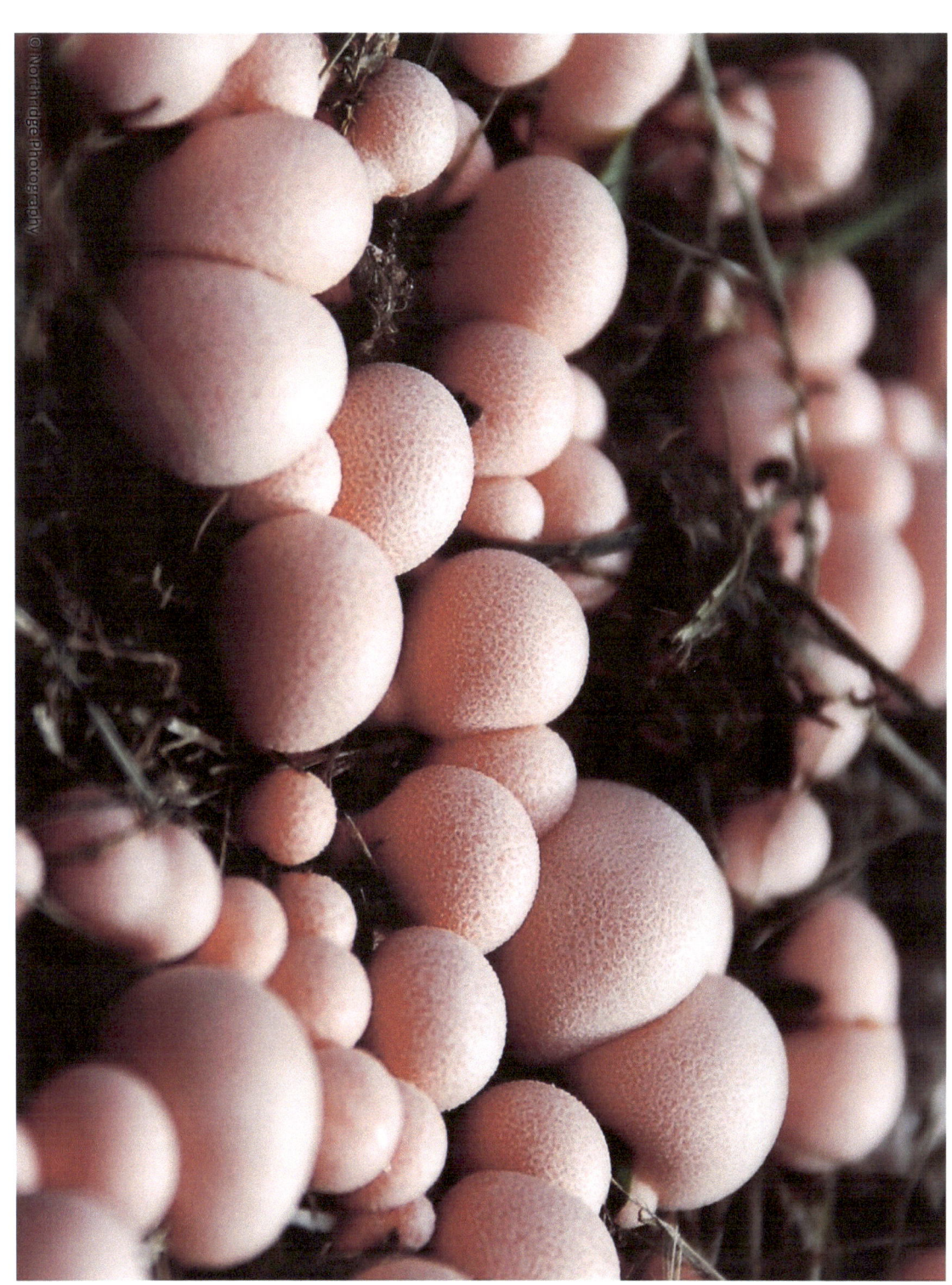
Balloon Rally

Waterway

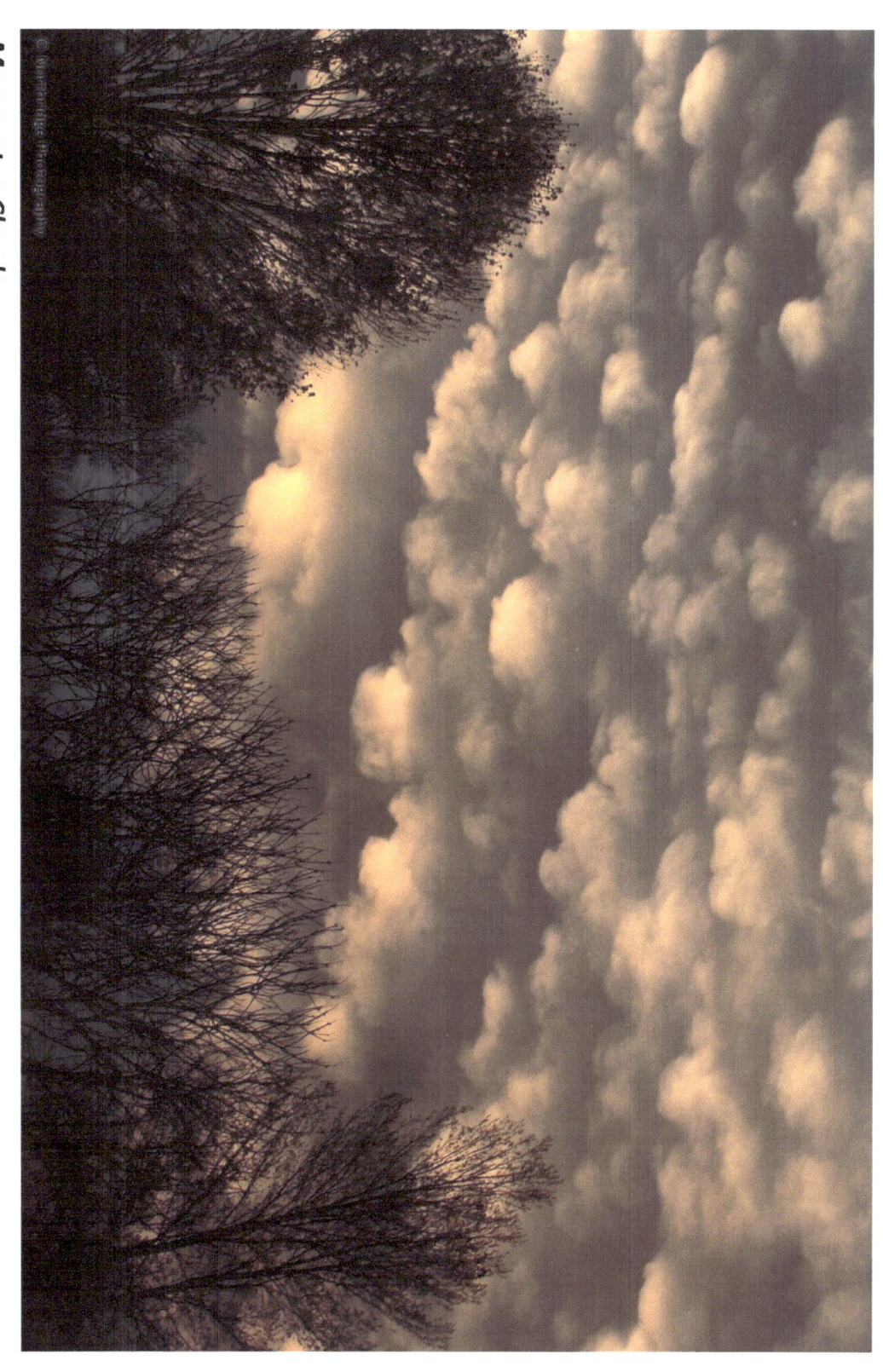

Mammatus Clouds

© Northridge Photography

Chickadee

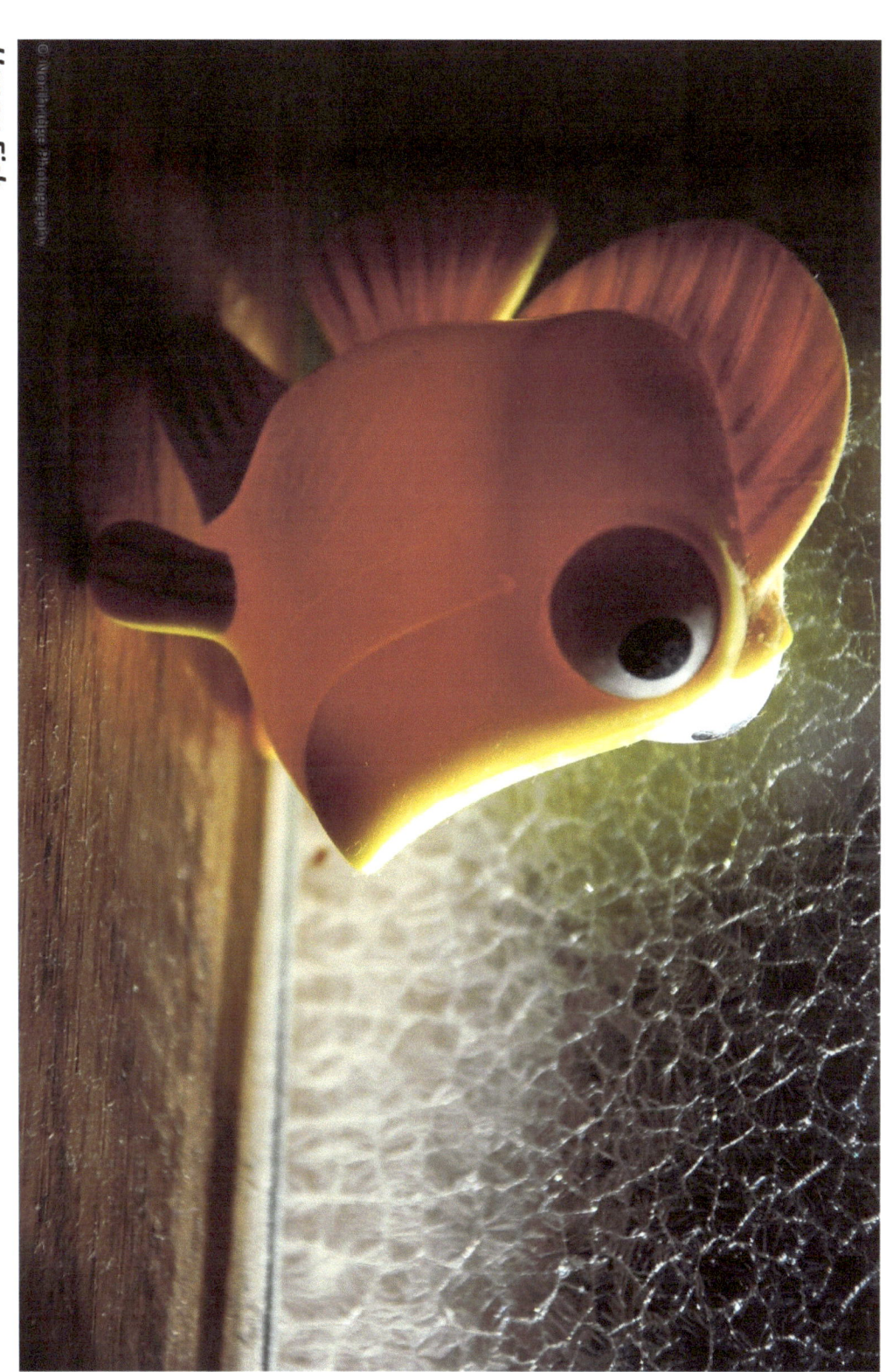
Happy Fish

Vivid

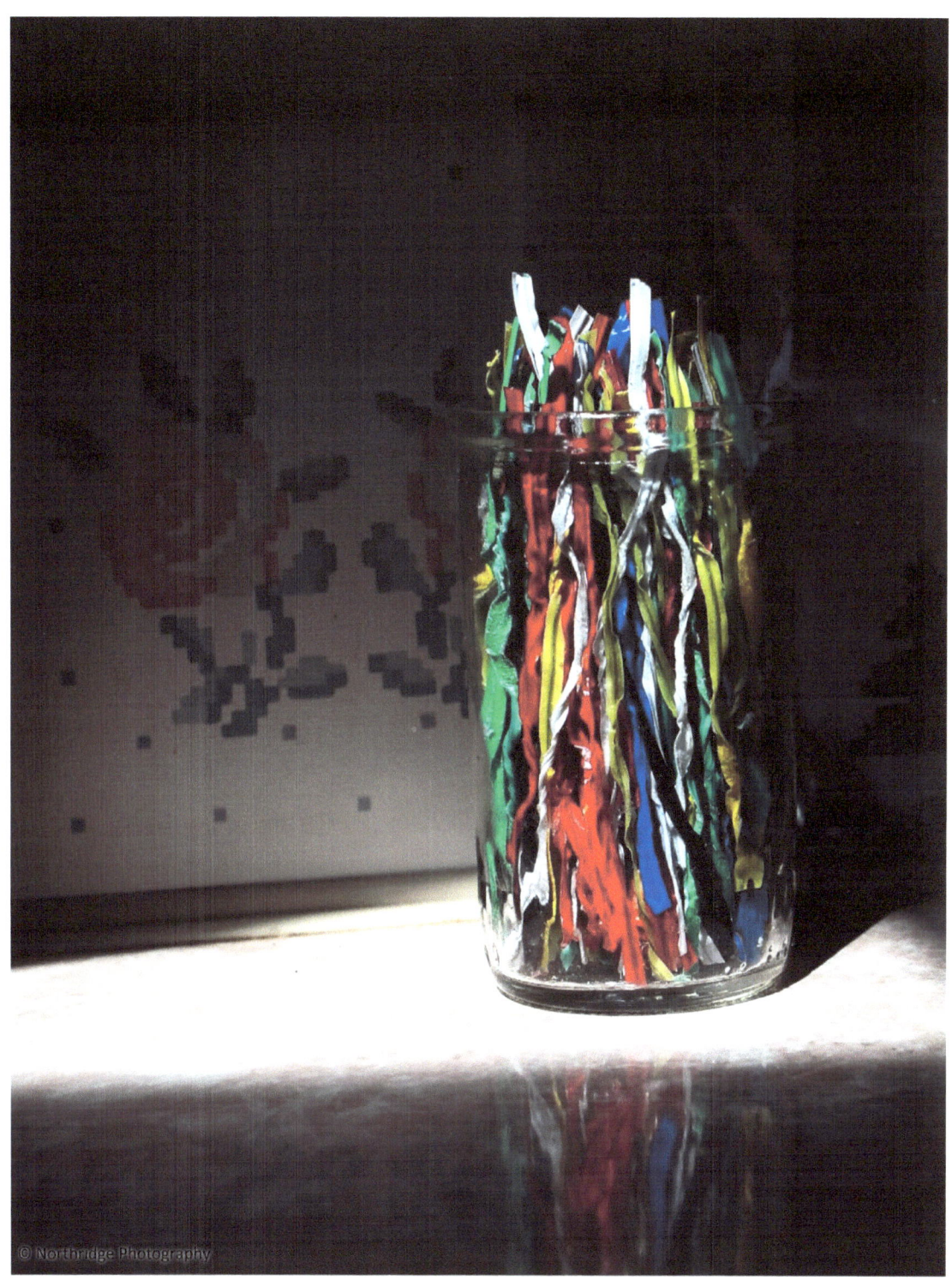

Collection

Water-Drum © Northbridge Photography

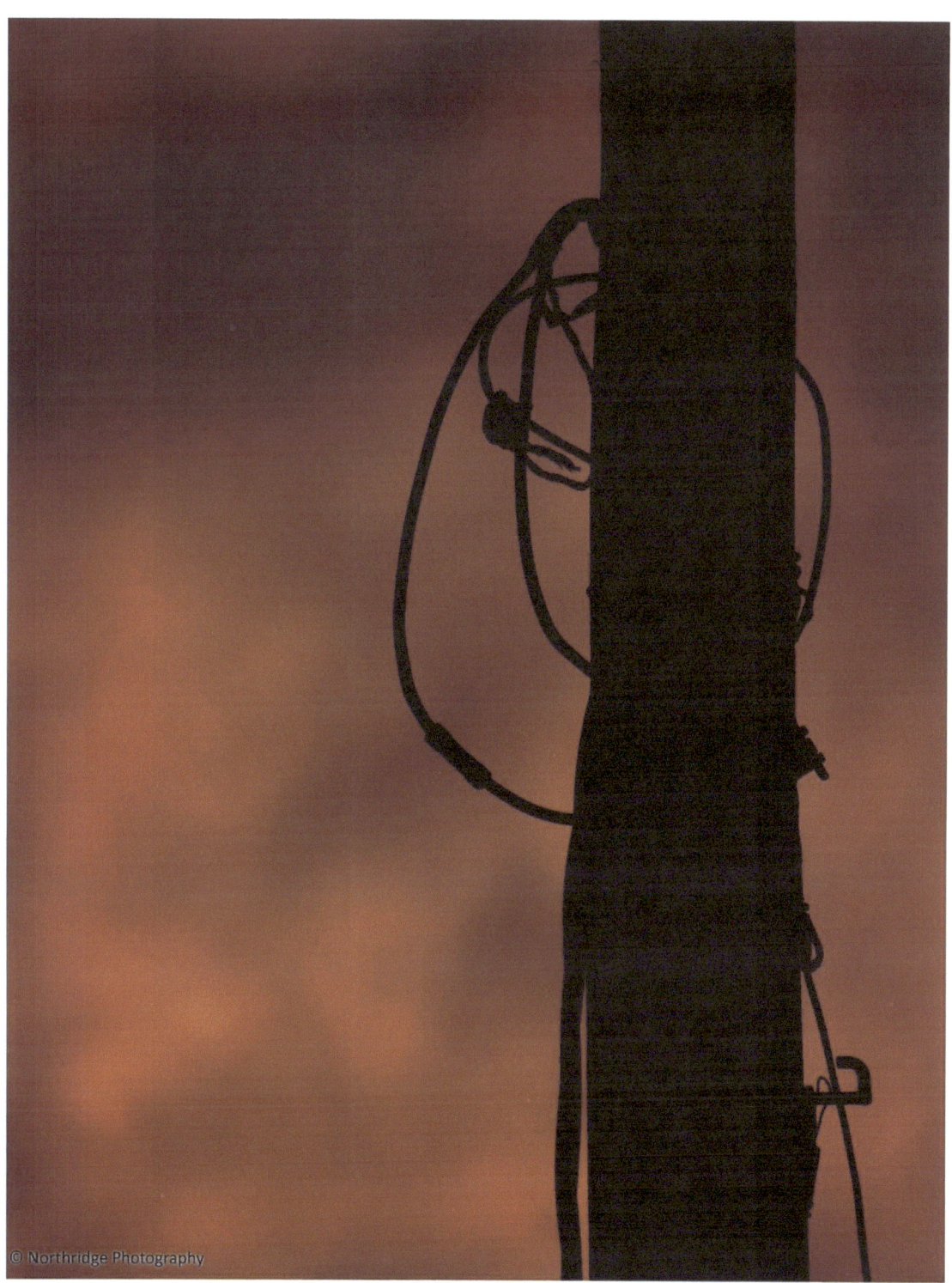

Done for the Night

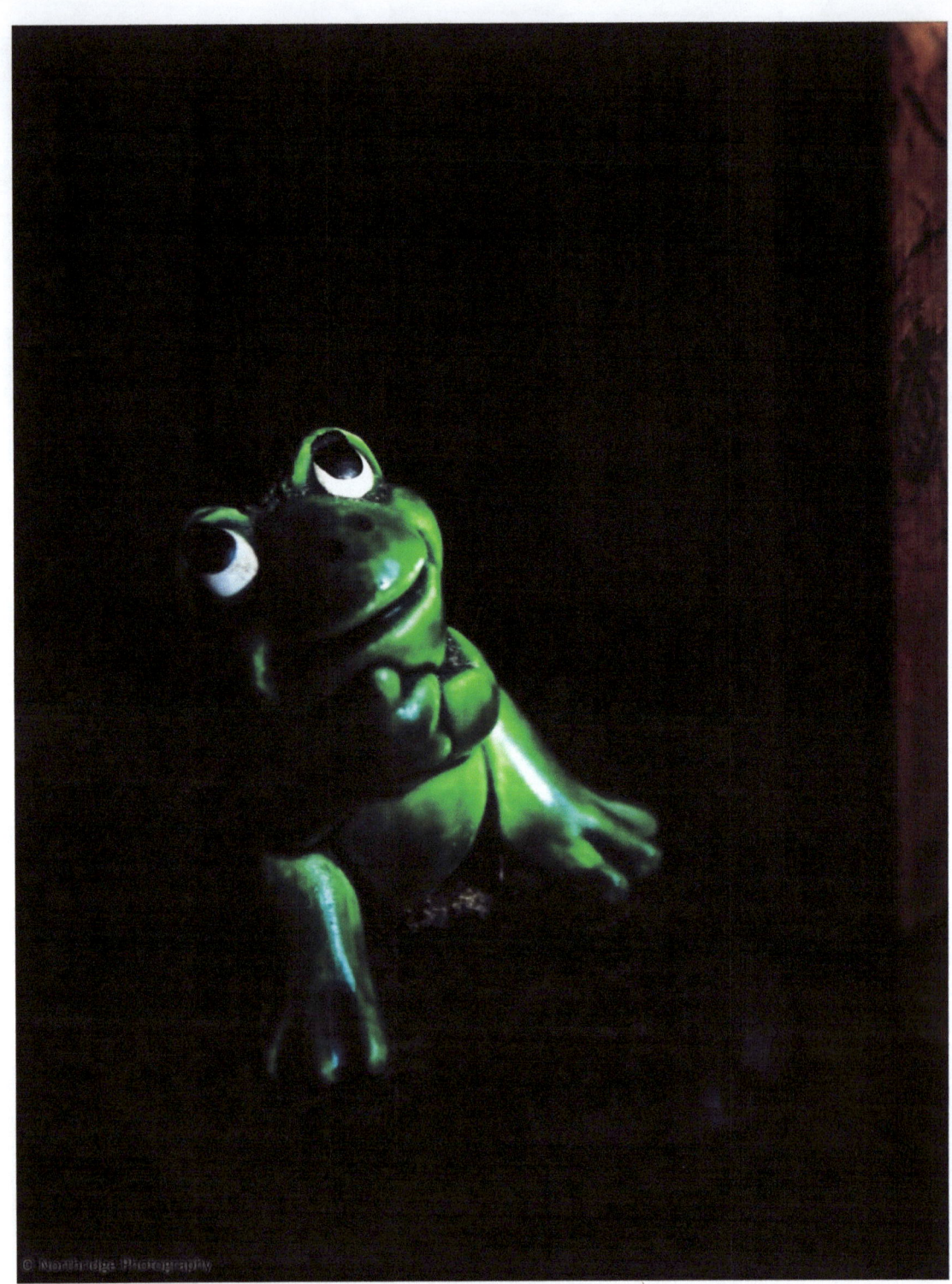

Please

www.ingramcontent.com/pod-product-compliance
Lightning Source LLC
Chambersburg PA
CBHW051200220526
45473CB00003B/848